THE OUTDOOR DUTCH OVEN COOKBOOK

THE OUTDOOR
DUTCH
OVEN
COOKBOOK

SHEILA MILLS

Ragged Mountain Press
Camden, Maine

International Marine/
Ragged Mountain Press

A Division of The McGraw-Hill Companies

10 9 8 7 6 5 4 3

Copyright © 1997 Ragged Mountain Press

Library of Congress Cataloging-in-Publication Data
Mills, Sheila.
        The outdoor dutch oven cookbook / Sheila Mills.
          p.   cm.
        Includes index.
        ISBN 0-07-043023-3
        1. Dutch oven cookery.   2. Outdoor cookery.   I. Title.
TX840.D88M55   1997
641.5'89––dc21   97-6193
                                                                                      CIP

Questions regarding the content of this book should be addressed to:

Ragged Mountain Press
P.O. Box 220
Camden, ME 04843

Questions regarding the ordering of this book should be addressed to:

McGraw-Hill, Inc.
Customer Service Department
P.O. Box 547
Blacklick, OH 43004
Retail customers: 1-800-262-4729
Bookstores: 1-800-233-4726

A portion of the profits from the sale of each Ragged Mountain Press book is donated to an environmental cause.

♲ This book is printed on 60-pound Renew Opaque Vellum, an acid-free paper that contains 50 percent recycled waste paper (preconsumer) and 10 percent postconsumer waste paper.

The Outdoor Dutch Oven Cookbook was set in Sabon, Gill Sans, and Engravers Bold
Printed by R.R. Donnelley & Sons, Crawfordsville, IN
Illustration on page 6 by Ruth Osterhout. All other illustrations by Parry Merkley
Design and Production by Dan Kirchoff
Edited by Jonathan Eaton; Elise Bauman; Kathryn Mallien

CONTENTS

ACKNOWLEDGMENTS

A special thanks to Shelley Thompson Cole, my administrative assistant, for her patience, persistence, and perfection.

To my friends and dedicated Dutch oven chefs who contributed recipes, and also to those of you who shared with David and me the results of recipe testing.

To Jim Brock, Rapid Creek Water Works, aquatic ecologist, inventor, river guide, and friend, for his enthusiastic support and for taking the time out of his busy schedule to help me write the section on low-impact camping.

To Harrison Hilbert, river guide and friend, for planting the seed to include tips on camp kitchen ethics and camp standards, whether in your backyard or on a riverbank in the wilderness.

To Jerry Myers, owner and operator of Silver Cloud Expeditions on the wilderness section of the Main Salmon River in Idaho, many thanks for contributing the section on catch-and-release fishing.

To Ruth Osterhout, a good friend and talented artist, for the dishwater-strainer sketch.

To all the Rocky Mountain River Tours guides who have cheerfully and meticulously followed my in-depth menus, giving the recipes a real test.

INTRODUCTION

All of the recipes in this book are geared to cooking outdoors. They can, however, be easily adapted to indoor cooking. The recipes have been tested at home in a conventional kitchen as well as outdoors in a Dutch oven. The Dutch oven is an ancient cooking tool, and I hope to keep it alive for many years to come.

David, my husband, and I operate Rocky Mountain River Tours, an outfitting business on the Middle Fork of the Salmon River in Idaho's Frank Church River of No Return Wilderness. We are fortunate to be able to share this beautiful country with people from all over the world, who come to float the river with us and our crew for a week's vacation. Part of this unforgettable experience for our guests is observing the creation of and dining on the exceptional meals prepared in Dutch ovens in a Rocky Mountain outdoor setting.

I think most people like to try something new. Buy a Dutch oven, try these recipes, and then adapt them to create your own meals. I hope you will enjoy the results and that this book will prove exciting and helpful.

If you are interested in experiencing truly excellent Dutch oven cooking in one of the most pristine wilderness environments in the world, you are invited to write to Rocky Mountain River Tours for a brochure on excursions on the Middle Fork of the Salmon River in Idaho.

Write or call Rocky Mountain River Tours, P.O. Box 2552, Boise, ID, 83701, (208)345-2400.

DUTCH OVEN CARE AND USE

The Dutch oven is a versatile cooking pot that substitutes for a host of outdoor cooking utensils. With its snug-fitting lid in place, it becomes an oven when heated with charcoal briquettes. Food can be baked, braised, stewed, or roasted. With the lid removed, the oven becomes a kettle for boiling, deep-fat frying, or heating food quickly over a fire. Even the lid doubles in service—it can be converted into a frying pan.

A true camp Dutch oven is easily identified by its legs, which extend below the oven and permit it to sit over hot coals, and its flat lid, which has a vertical lip around the outside edge to retain the hot coals that are placed on top.

There are several types of Dutch ovens on the market. The camp Dutch oven is not regularly stocked by supermarkets and hardware stores, so you may need to order it directly from the manufacturer or a river supply or outdoor equipment catalog. The important thing to watch for when purchasing a Dutch oven for outdoor use is that it is not simply a flat-bottomed kettle made for kitchen cooking. If you plan to prepare the recipes at home using a conventional oven and stove, a flat-bottomed Dutch oven will suffice.

The camp Dutch oven is made specifically for outdoor cooking. It is made of heavy cast iron or aluminum, and comes in basic sizes from 8 to 24 inches in diameter, and from 4 to 6 inches deep.

The cast iron Dutch oven is heavy, thick, and flat on the bottom, with three short legs. The lid is tight-fitting and has a vertical lip with a handle in the center. There also is a bail for lifting the entire unit. Proper seasoning of a cast iron camp Dutch oven is essential. If you scour your oven with strong detergents, it will need reseasoning frequently. Rub the oven with unsalted shortening and place it in a 400°F oven until it smokes and then wipe out the excess fat. If you are camping, just place it on the coals with the lid on until it smokes. Then wipe it out. If you wash it with detergent between uses, it is a good idea to oil it to keep it from rusting. It is best, too, to store a cast iron Dutch oven upside down and with the lid off.

The aluminum Dutch oven is popular with campers because it is lightweight, rustproof, and requires no seasoning. However, cast iron, though it is heavier than aluminum and takes longer to heat, heats evenly and stays hot for a long period of time. It is important that you do not overheat an aluminum oven, because you can damage it permanently. The aluminum Dutch is one-third the weight of the cast iron, and thus it is more portable on camping trips. It is the only model that can be backpacked by a hiker. The two types cost about the same.

Use charcoal briquettes to heat your Dutch oven, allowing twenty to thirty minutes for them to heat properly before placing them around the oven. It is a good idea to preheat the lid when baking, to prevent heat from being drawn out of the porous iron by cold ingredients.

Most of the following recipes are adapted for six to eight servings and can be prepared in a 10" or 12" oven. An aluminum oven heats quickly and requires five to eight briquettes evenly distributed underneath and twelve to sixteen briquettes on the lid for a 12" oven. Using additional coals to try to speed up the cooking time is unwise, since it can damage the aluminum and cause the food to burn.

Cast iron requires more cooking time than aluminum, but the number of coals on top and bottom remains the same. Either the cast iron or aluminum Dutch oven can be permanently damaged by pouring cold water into a hot oven; by uneven heating caused by putting coals on only half the oven or lid; by careless packing while traveling (the legs can be broken off or pushed up through the bottom by too much jamming); and by rust and corrosion.

The lid, turned upside down on the coals, can be used for frying. When using more than one oven, the second can be stacked on top of the first, and so on.

When checking for doneness, do not leave the lid off any longer than necessary. It is equivalent to opening your oven door at home—you will lose all the heat. It is very important that the lid remain tightly sealed.

The original camp Dutch oven evolved through centuries of experience. It was designed for cooking complete meals on open fires without the need for other appliances (a shovel, pliers, and leather gloves come in handy, though). It is at once a kettle, a frying pan, an oven, a pot, and a stove—all in one portable utensil.

A unique cooking device, the Dutch oven can produce delicious and nutritious meals with little trouble or skill. To demonstrate the talents of the camp Dutch oven, I have included recipes for a variety of dishes in this cookbook. If you are not acquainted with an authentic camp Dutch oven, I suggest you make friends with one right away. Use your oven to prepare leisurely campsite meals, and then settle back and enjoy some of the most delectable dishes you have ever eaten.

THE COOKING ENVIRONMENT

A few simple rules of conduct can help contribute to low-impact cooking in camp and the perpetuation of beautiful, natural campsite environments. Things to consider for low-impact cooking include the following:

Gas Stoves

Use whenever possible, especially in areas where fire danger is high, driftwood is scarce, (i.e. on desert rivers or during drought years), and anytime on popular, high-use rivers.

Efficient propane stoves are favored by many boaters.

A 2½-gallon propane cylinder provides adequate fuel for a party of fifteen for a six-day trip, with the stove used for about half of the cooking tasks and the remainder done with charcoal on a grill or in Dutch ovens (this does not include heating wash water on the stove).

Charcoal Briquettes

Provide consistent, long-lasting heat.

Reduce the impact of wood gathering around campsites.

Result in minimal ash residue.

A 10-pound bag of briquettes will provide cooking heat for six Dutch ovens, which will serve thirty people.

Firepans and Ashes

A firepan can be made from sheet metal with 3- to 4-inch sides to contain ashes.

Oil drain pans, which are available from auto parts stores, make excellent firepans for small groups. The round pans have 3- to 4-inch sides, nest together, and are a perfect size for a Dutch oven.

Firepans eliminate proliferation of unsightly fire rings and reduce the demand for wood, because users tend to build smaller fires.

Use of a firepan helps prevent wildfires.

Firepans are required on many rivers.

Firepans prevent the spread of ash or charcoal on beaches and in camps.

Elevate your firepan on rocks, if possible, to protect the soil and surrounding vegetation. If you are not able to elevate it, put it on bare sand or a gravel bar, where it will do the least damage to soil organisms.

Each morning before breaking camp, some groups turn their cookfire into a refuse incinerator. Burning garbage, especially plastics, in the cookfire produces objectionable smoke and fumes. I recommend packing your plastic, aluminum, and paper products and food scraps for recycling or disposal at a designated landfill.

Manage your campfire to produce the least amount of residue.

After your fire has burned completely down, stir into the embers a small amount of water, unused coffee, or dishwater.

Transfer mixture into an airtight surplus ammo can or a similar metal container. Bring enough cans to contain such residue for your group for the entire trip.

At your next campsite, recycle the ash to cover the bottom of your firepan, which will reduce the ash further and eliminate warping of the pan.

Do not dump residue into rivers or streams, because it will be deposited back onto the beaches and banks.

The environmental impact along streams and river corridors is significantly reduced by the use of firepans and low-impact camping.

Etiquette for Gathering and Burning Firewood

Never cut or burn live vegetation.

Use downed or dead wood that you can break by hand for fuel. Standing dead wood is part of the natural setting and provides a natural habitat for birds and small animals.

Do not bring hazardous, thorny, or sharp pieces of wood into the camp area for use as fuel.

Never collect firewood that is thicker than your forearm.

Keep your fire as small as possible.

Designate an area to break wood for fire fuel, and make sure this area is left looking natural before departing camp.

Your firepan should be located in a level, safe area, where the flames or heat will not ignite overhead branches or nearby objects.

You might want to designate a member of your group to be responsible for a safe, efficient campfire.

Gloves, pliers, a shovel, and shoes are essential for your protection and convenience in working with the fire and charcoal.

Do not build your campfire bigger than necessary.

There is generally no need for an ax or saw for firewood preparation.

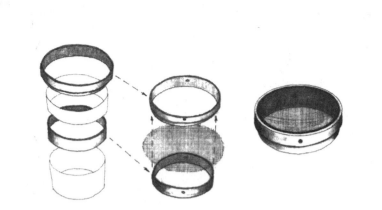

RUTH OSTERHOUT

Making a dishwater strainer.

Disposal of Waste Water

Never pour unused juices or fluids on the ground or in a stream, as they may attract flies, yellowjackets, chipmunks, and bears. Pour them into your garbage container (an airtight, 20-mm ammo can) if camping on a river. Some of the fluid can also be poured into the lower edge of your firepan, where it will boil off.

Never pour waste water or fluids into an outhouse, because it retards biodegradation. Fecal material in a pit privy must be dry to reach the necessary 140°F temperature in order to biodegrade.

Strain dishwater above the highwater level and far away from camp. Put solid particles in your trash container.

A strainer can be made with a piece of window screen stretched over a ring cut from a 5-gallon plastic bucket. Cut two rings from a tapered bucket, which will interlock around the screen when pushed together. Secure with pop rivets (see illustration).

Strain the first wash bucket first and use the last rinse to wash down the others.

Camp/River Sanitation

In order to prevent contamination of food and water when camping, personal and environmental cleanliness are vitally important. All backcountry water should be considered potentially contaminated by *Giardia* or some other harmful microorganism. When carrying water is not practical, you will have to kill or remove the disease-causing organisms by heat, chemical, or mechanical disinfection of the water. Water purification is a complex subject, and you should consult a reliable source for detailed information.

Along wilderness rivers where human contamination is minimal, a water filter (those featuring a cleanable ceramic candle are recommended), is ideal for preparing water for drinking and food preparation. These filters are available at most river supply companies and some sporting goods stores. Large water containers can be filled in camp and carried on rafts or boats for easy access to fresh water. Remember to disinfect drinking water containers on a regular basis.

Chlorine bleach is commonly used as a disinfectant.

Two inexpensive items are important to have on hand for a camping trip where you are using water from nearby streams. They are chlorine bleach and chlorine litmus papers, available at any spa or restaurant supply store. (Sanitizing rinses should be 50–100 ppm chlorine according to State Health Department regulations.)

Use 1½ to 2 tablespoons of chlorine bleach per 5-gallon bucket of water.

After 15 minutes, use the chlorine test paper to check water.

The effectiveness of chlorine varies with temperature and turbidity of the water source.

The only acceptable way to carry garbage is in an airtight metal or plastic container.

DAN KIRCHOFF

A handwash bucket.

Carrying garbage in a plastic bag alone is inadequate because the bags tear easily and are impossible to secure to a boat to prevent loss in case of an accident.

Have a 5-gallon handwash bucket available at all meals for the cooks and everyone who is sharing the food. For each handwash bucket, use an 8-ounce plastic measuring cup with an open handle to hang on the side of the bucket, with a small hole drilled in the bottom to dispense the water. Add 1½ to 2 tablespoons of bleach per 5-gallon bucket of water, as mentioned above. To wash hands, fill the measuring cup with bleach-water and hang by handle over the edge of the bucket;

wash hands as water flows from the hole in the bottom of the cup. Do not use this handwash bucket to wash food.

No one with the symptoms of a communicable disease, especially diarrhea, should be allowed to prepare food or handle utensils for other people.

Insist that everyone wash their hands with soap and water after using the toilet. Follow the same disinfecting procedure for the handwash bucket, as stated above.

Scrape food residue with a rubber spatula from plates and Dutch ovens into your garbage container. This helps keep dishwater cleaner.

To wash dishes, use buckets that can be heated on the fire or stove. (Use three buckets of water heated to boiling, with 1½ to 2 tablespoons of bleach per 5-gallon bucket for sanitizing.)

Wash Dutch ovens and cooking pots last to avoid fouling the wash and rinse water.

The final rinse temperature should be too hot to immerse your hands in the water.

Nondisposable plates are very handy on camping trips and do not create garbage the way paper ones do. Use plates at all meals to prevent food droppings. No food or watermelon seeds should be left on the ground to attract insects and small animals. Remember that popular campsites are occupied every night and can be impacted by careless camp practices.

Use only knives from the kitchen kit for food preparation. These should be washed after each meal. Personal knives should not be used in food preparation, especially folding knives, which harbor bacteria.

Separate your glass and aluminum bottles and cans from the rest of your trash. These can be recycled in most cities.

Human Waste Disposal

Because of the impact on soils, vegetation, and hazards associated with burial of feces, on some rivers human wastes should be packed into a collection container specified for this use or a sanitary landfill or RV dump station. This type of "pack it out" policy for fecal material is a requirement for boaters on the Colorado River's Grand Canyon. A procedure that has proved effective on such rivers is to use a 20-mm airtight ammo can fitted with a toilet seat. Plastic seats molded especially to fit on ammo cans are available in fashion colors from river equipment suppliers. Use a deodorant chemical. Have a water dispenser and soap available for handwashing.

In remote locations where toilets are unavailable and "pack it out" practices for human waste are not needed, feces should be disposed of in a place where they will not pollute water and will not be found by others. The recommended policy currently emphasizes burial of human feces in small latrines ("catholes") located at least 300 feet from the nearest surface water. Group use of single latrines at overnight campsites is not generally recommended since such concentration of human waste tends to increase the health hazard.

Practice No-Kill, Catch-and-Release Fishing
by Jerry Myers

Trout fishing is becoming one of America's fastest-growing outdoor sports and an important activity of many river users. Unfortunately, our trout streams, and the trout populations sustained by these streams, are finite. Many streams contain unique subspecies of trout that do not exist elsewhere. Killing wild trout, regardless of local regulations, is not a viable option if we want to insure quality fishing in years to come. We do not have to give up fishing, nor do we have to witness a decline in the fishing quality of our favorite streams. We do, however, have to practice proper, no-kill, catch-and-release fishing methods. Regardless of how carefully we catch and release trout, a certain number will die. The following tips will help keep fish mortality to a minimum:

Use a single barbless hook of the proper size. If your hooks are barbed, simply pinch the barb down flat with needlenose pliers or fishing forceps. Break or cut off two hooks on lures with treble hoods and pinch the barb on the remaining hook. Hooks that are too large for the fish you are catching can pierce the brain or the eyes of the fish.

Limit the time you play the fish. A hooked fish builds lactic acid in its tissues that can cause shock and even death. Excessively light tackle extends landing time and can overstress the fish. Use adequate tackle.

Limit your handling of the fish. Use fishing forceps or a hook disgorger to remove the hook, and leave the fish in the water, if possible. Do not squeeze the fish or handle it by the gills or gill covers. Never pick up a trout by its gills or by its lower jaw. If you must handle a fish, do it over the water, not in a boat or over the shore. If you cannot handle a fish in or over the water, you are in the wrong position. Change it.

If the hook is in the fish's throat, or is difficult to remove, cut the line as close to the hook as possible and release the fish. The hook will rust out quickly. If you must use a net, leave the netted fish in the water. Choose a net of soft cotton or nylon netting.

Exhausted fish should be gently held in swimming position under water until the fish is able to swim away under its own power. A gentle back and forth movement will help it breathe; or hold it so that it is facing upstream in the current.

If you want a photograph of the fish, make sure it is revived, and leave it in the water until your camera is ready. Gently grasp the fish just in front of the tail fin and support the fish's body by placing your other hand under its belly. Larger fish require more support when lifting. Never grab for the fish if it slips from your hands, and always handle the fish over the water. You can get beautiful photographs and still leave the fish in the water by simply turning the fish onto its side on the surface of the water. Never drop or throw a fish back into the water.

Remember that every fish you hook is at risk. Trying to catch as many fish as you can, as fast as you can, will result in higher mortality rates. Take time to enjoy the many other aspects of fishing. You may want to fish with a hookless fly or lure. Often the greatest satisfaction is getting a fish to take a fly or lure, not necessarily setting the hook. Teach others the importance of wild fish and proper, no-kill, catch-and-release practices.

Jerry Myers, Silver Cloud Expeditions of Salmon, Idaho, is a fishing and river outfitter on the Wild Salmon River, and is one of Idaho's top authorities on fishing.

Keeping Food Cold and Fresh

Ice chest performance is affected by numerous factors, including air temperature, cooler insulating capacity, the ratio of food to ice, and the frequency and conditions under which the chest is opened. Compared to small coolers, large ice chests generally are better insulated and have more favorable surface-to-volume ratios, which means they will keep food colder longer using the same amount of ice as smaller coolers.

Unless special precautions are taken (such as supplementing water ice with a block of dry ice in a "deep freeze" meat cooler), midsummer boaters can expect that their ice supplies will be exhausted after about a week under ideal operation. That time can be cut in half if the cooler is operated poorly.

An approach to ice chest management favored by some boaters is to dedicate one or more coolers for the second half of their first week. For example, all perishable foods for days four through six might be packed in one chest and taped shut. In addition to extending the chilling capacity by cutting down on cooler opening, this approach can save time searching for food items during the first half of the trip. River scientist J. T. Brock has collected data on cooler performance under outfitted river trip conditions. In these studies, a 151-quart Igloo ice chest was wired with probes and a portable computer that recorded air, water, and internal cooler temperatures at the bottom, middle, and top of the chest. The study documented the presence of substantial temperature gradients within the ice chests. Four days into a July trip on the Middle Fork of the Salmon River, with maximum air temperatures in the low 90s, while block ice was chilling the bottom of the cooler to 34°F, the temperature at the top of the cooler approached 70°F. This thermal stratification should be borne in mind when positioning foods in an ice chest; place especially perishable or heat-sensitive items close to the ice at the bottom of the chest.

Block ice aged at sub-zero temperatures

is preferable for extended camping trips, because it lasts longer.

To avoid unnecessary opening, label each cooler, using a felt-tip marker, which can be washed off at the end of the trip.

The Complete Camp and River Kitchen

Firepan

Cooking grate with adjustable legs (to fit inside firepan)

Dutch ovens, saucepans, and skillets, as needed for the menu

Pancake griddle

Water filter (if not cleanable, take along a spare cartridge)

Galvanized metal buckets for dishwashing

Handwash buckets (plastic), with dispensing plastic measuring cups

Soap for washing dishes and hands

Chlorine bleach

Coffee pot(s)

Shovel

Gas stove (preferably propane or white gas)

Spice kit

Screened dishwater strainer

Cups (reusable), with storage bag

Plates (reusable), with storage bag

Eating utensils (metal), with storage bag

Portable table with oilcloth or vinyl tablecloth

Cutting boards (absorbent wood should not be used)

Mixing bowls

Culinary knives with blade guards

Hard plastic and rubber spatulas

Cooking utensils (as needed for your menu)

Sponges and scrubbers

Compartmentalized canvas roll-up bag for utensils

Wooden matches in waterproof container or butane fire igniter

Charcoal briquettes and lighter fluid

Corkscrew, can opener, and bottle opener

Thermos or airpot for coffee, tea, and/or hot water

Cloth dishtowels

Work gloves

Time-Saving Tips

When baking breads and cakes, line your Dutch oven with parchment or baker's paper to prevent sticking. Cut the paper into rounds to fit your Dutch oven. Parchment is available at any bakery. When the recipe calls for a pastry dough, you can use a commercially packaged crust, such as Krusteaz Pie Crust Mix, my favorite.

To save on knife blades and on time, purchase canned foods that are already chopped, such as black olives and green chiles.

Wash produce prior to your trip. Spin-dry the lettuce and leafy green vegetables and put them in a zip-top bag with a paper towel. They will keep for a week in a cooler.

Premeasure and mix the dry ingredients for cakes and breads and put them in labeled zip-top bags prior to your trip.

Prepare salad dressings, dips, and sauces in advance and put them in sealed containers.

If you are going to serve a pasta salad, make it ahead of time if it is to be used in a day or two. If it won't be served until later in the trip, you can still cook the pasta in advance.

Slice, grate, and chop food items in advance to take advantage of your food processor at home and save time on your trip. You also have less waste to deal with on the trail.

Portion out meat and other items, heat-seal them in plastic bags, and freeze them in advance of your trip.

It helps to make a menu listing the items used so that all the people involved in your trip can assist in meal preparation.

Pack items into your cooler(s) according to when they will be used. Mark coolers and other storage containers as to their contents.

Use a wine bottle to roll out dough.

Carry utensils in a sealed, plastic container and take several hand towels to avoid using paper towels.

Resources for "The Cooking Environment":

Meyer, Kathleen. How to Shit in the Woods: An Environmentally Sound Approach to a Lost Art. *Ten Speed Press: Berkeley, California, 1989.*

Cole, David N. Low-Impact Recreational Practices for Wilderness and Backcountry. *U.S. Department of Agriculture Forest Service Intermountain Research Station, Ogden, Utah. General Technical Report INT-265, 1989.*

BREAKFAST DISHES

REMEMBER

When a recipe calls for baking, braising, stewing, or roasting, the Dutch oven must be covered with charcoal briquettes on top of the lid. For boiling, frying, sautéing, and quick-heating, leave the Dutch oven cover off. For more on cooking techniques for the Dutch oven, see "Dutch Oven Care and Use," pages 2–3.

EGGS ELEGANT

½ teaspoon salt
¼ teaspoon pepper
1 tablespoon dry mustard
2 cans (10½ ounces each) cream of
    chicken soup
1 cup milk
8 ounces grated Cheddar cheese (2 cups)
1 package (10 ounces) frozen asparagus
    pieces, thawed and drained
8 eggs
4 whole wheat English muffins

Combine salt, pepper, dry mustard, cream of chicken soup, and milk in Dutch oven or saucepan. Stir over medium heat until smooth and creamy. Stir in cheese until melted. Add asparagus pieces.

If cooking in Dutch oven, make hollows for six to eight eggs; break an egg into each hollow. For conventional cooking, pour egg mixture into 9"x 11" casserole dish.

Bake in Dutch oven for 15 to 20 minutes, or in 350°F conventional oven for 30 minutes (or until eggs are set to your liking).

Cut English muffins in half and toast. Serve eggs over English muffins, one egg to each half.

Yield: 8 servings

SKOOKUMCHUCK SCRAMBLED EGGS

These eggs are named for a creek flowing into the Salmon River. Skookumchuck means "strong rapid."

⅓ cup minced scallions
¼ green pepper, seeded and minced
2 tablespoons butter
24 eggs, well beaten
¼ cup imitation bacon bits
2 tablespoons dried parsley flakes
¼ cup milk
8 ounces Cheddar cheese, grated (2 cups)

Sauté scallions and green pepper in butter in Dutch oven until tender. Add beaten eggs, bacon bits, and parsley, and mix well. Stir frequently until eggs are cooked. Add milk and cheese and stir until cheese melts. Serve immediately.

Yield: 10 to 12 servings

EGGS BENEDICT

8 eggs
4 English muffins
8 thin slices ham, broiled or Canadian
    bacon
1 recipe Jiffy Hollandaise sauce (see page
    72) or 1 package dry instant
    Hollandaise sauce
1 teaspoon paprika

Poach eggs. (If using a Dutch oven, fill half full with water and bring to a boil. Remove from heat. Add eggs to water and replace lid on Dutch oven for 3 to 5 minutes.)

Split and toast the English muffins. Top each half with a thin slice of broiled ham or Canadian bacon. Place a poached egg on the ham.

Prepare Hollandaise sauce and pour over all. Sprinkle with paprika and serve immediately.

Yield: 8 servings

FANCY EGG SCRAMBLE

Cheese Sauce:

2 tablespoons butter
2 tablespoons flour
$\frac{1}{2}$ teaspoon salt
$\frac{1}{8}$ teaspoon pepper
2 cups milk
4 ounces Cheddar cheese, grated (1 cup)

Egg Scramble:

1 cup diced Canadian bacon
$\frac{1}{3}$ cup chopped scallions
$\frac{1}{4}$ pound fresh mushrooms, sliced
3 tablespoons butter
12 eggs, well beaten
4 teaspoons butter, melted
$2\frac{1}{4}$ cups bread crumbs (or 3 slices bread,
    grated)
$\frac{1}{8}$ teaspoon paprika

Make the cheese sauce: Melt butter in a saucepan. Blend in flour, salt, and pepper. Add milk. Cook, stirring all the while, until bubbly. Stir in Cheddar cheese and cook until melted. Set aside.

In Dutch oven or skillet, cook Canadian bacon, scallions, and mushrooms in butter until onion is tender but not brown. Add eggs and scramble until just set.

Fold eggs into cheese sauce. Pour into Dutch oven or 9"x 11" casserole dish.

In a separate bowl combine the melted butter, crumbs, and paprika; sprinkle over eggs.

Cover Dutch oven and bake for 15 minutes; remove top coals and bake slowly from bottom another 10 minutes. Or bake in 375°F conventional oven for 15 minutes.

Yield: 8 to 10 servings

AVOCADO FRITTATA

1 tablespoon unsalted butter
2 tablespoons olive oil
1 small onion, chopped
1 garlic clove, minced
½ teaspoon salt
freshly ground black pepper to taste
½ teaspoon dried basil
½ teaspoon dried oregano
6 eggs, well beaten
2 avocados, sliced
4 ounces Cheddar cheese, grated (1 cup)
salsa for topping

Heat butter and olive oil in 10" Dutch oven or oven-proof skillet over medium heat. Sauté onion and garlic. Add salt, pepper, basil, and oregano.

Increase heat to high and pour in eggs, letting the uncooked egg flow under vegetables as you would for an omelet. Reduce the heat to medium. Top with avocados and cheese.

Cover pan. For Dutch oven, use coals on top and bottom and bake for 10 minutes or until the frittata is firm. For conventional cooking, put pan in 400°F oven and bake for 10 minutes or until firm. Cut in wedges to serve. Top with salsa.

Yield: 6 servings

ROCKY MOUNTAIN EGGS

This breakfast surprise turns scrambled eggs into a sturdy entree.

2 tablespoons plus 4 tablespoons butter
   or margarine
2 small potatoes, cut into ½-inch cubes
1 large onion, finely chopped
8 ounces ground spicy turkey sausage
2 tablespoons chopped fresh parsley
6 eggs
½ teaspoon salt
freshly ground black pepper to taste
1 tablespoon milk
2 ounces Monterey Jack cheese, grated
   (½ cup)

Heat 2 tablespoons butter in Dutch oven. Sauté potatoes, onion, and sausage for about 15 minutes until sausage is browned evenly and potatoes are tender. Sprinkle with parsley and dot with 4 tablespoons butter, and reduce heat.

In a separate bowl, beat eggs with salt, pepper, and milk. Pour into Dutch oven over cooked ingredients and cook, lifting set portion with a spatula to let uncooked egg flow underneath. When nearly set, sprinkle with cheese and cover until cheese melts. Cut into wedges to serve.

Yield: 4 to 6 servings

VEGETABLE EGG CUPS

These are delicious served for breakfast or brunch.

oil for greasing pan
6 frozen puff pastry shells
6 ounces Cheddar cheese, grated
    (1 1/2 cups)
3 tablespoons unbleached all-purpose
    flour
3 eggs, lightly beaten
1/4 cup chopped fresh mushrooms
1/4 cup chopped zucchini
3 tablespoons chopped onion
6 crisply cooked bacon slices, crumbled
1/2 teaspoon salt
dash pepper

Lightly grease 6 muffin cups, or use paper muffin cups.

Roll out each pastry shell into a 6- to 8-inch circle. Line each muffin cup with a circle of dough, so that the edges of the dough stand up at least a half inch above the cup edge.

Toss cheese with flour. Add eggs, mushrooms, zucchini, onion, bacon, salt, and pepper, and mix well. Fill the cups with the cheese mixture.

Bake in Dutch oven for 35 to 40 minutes, or in 350°F oven for 50 minutes.

Yield: 6 servings

HUEVOS MIDDLE FORK

1 teaspoon plus 2 tablespoons corn oil
6 corn tortillas, cut in half
12 eggs
4 large scallions, sliced
2 fresh jalapeño peppers, very thinly sliced
1/2 red bell pepper, diced
1/4 cup chopped cilantro
1 1/2 teaspoons ground cumin
4 ounces feta cheese, crumbled
salt and pepper to taste
cilantro sprigs for garnish

Heat 1 teaspoon oil, add tortilla halves, and fry until golden brown and crisp. Transfer to paper towels and drain.

Beat together eggs, scallions, jalapeño and bell peppers, cilantro, cumin, and half of the cheese. Crumble in four tortilla halves. Season to taste with salt and pepper. Let stand 5 minutes.

Heat 2 tablespoons oil and add egg mixture. Cook until just set, stirring frequently. Sprinkle with remaining cheese. Stand two tortilla halves in each serving and garnish with cilantro sprigs.

Yield: 4 servings

BREAKFAST QUESADILLAS

For a less spicy quesadilla, use smaller amounts of jalapeño and cayenne pepper.

Salsa:

4 plum tomatoes, quartered lengthwise
    and thinly sliced
1 small zucchini, quartered lengthwise and
    thinly sliced
⅔ yellow pepper, diced
4 scallions, thinly sliced
2 jalapeño peppers, seeded and minced
2 tablespoons minced cilantro
4 teaspoons lime juice, or more to taste
½ teaspoon lime zest
cayenne pepper to taste
¼ teaspoon salt

Assembly:

4 flour tortillas (8-inch size)
2 ounces Monterey Jack cheese, very
    finely grated
4 tablespoons sour cream
cilantro sprigs for garnish

Make the salsa: Stir together tomatoes, zucchini, yellow pepper, scallions, jalapeño, cilantro, lime juice and zest, cayenne pepper, and salt.

Warm a tortilla in a skillet for 1 to 2 minutes. Turn tortilla and spoon one quarter of the salsa over half of it. Top salsa with one quarter of the cheese, fold tortilla over filling, and cook until salsa is heated through and cheese has melted, 2 to 3 minutes. Transfer quesadilla to plate and keep warm in Dutch oven. Repeat with other tortillas. Serve topped with sour cream and sprigs of cilantro.

Yield: 4 servings

BREAKFAST FONDUE

This delicious breakfast dish recipe was given to me by my aunt, Mac Oliver, from Billings, Montana, where she serves it every year for Christmas brunch. If you are not camping, begin this recipe the night before you are to serve it. However, it can also be prepared to be served immediately.

butter for greasing pan
6 slices whole wheat bread, cubed
6 ounces Cheddar cheese, grated
    (1½ cups)
⅓ pound link sausage (can use bulk)
3 eggs
1⅔ cups milk
½ teaspoon dry mustard
¼ can cream of mushroom soup
⅓ cup milk

Butter a large casserole dish or Dutch oven. Place bread cubes in dish. Sprinkle with cheese. Brown the sausage, then drain and cut into thirds (or crumble if using bulk sausage). Place over cheese.

In a separate bowl, beat eggs slightly with milk and dry mustard. Pour egg mixture over sausage. Refrigerate overnight, unless you are camping.

Dilute soup with milk and pour over all. Bake in Dutch oven for about 1 hour, or bake in a 300°F oven for 1½ hours, until it is set.

Yield: 6 to 8 servings

CHILAQUILES

1 cup chopped red onion
1/2 cup chopped tomato
1 cup chopped Swiss chard
1 tablespoon vegetable oil
1/2 cup cooked corn
1/2 cup cooked black beans, drained and
    rinsed if canned
1 cup shredded cooked chicken
1/2 cup chicken broth
1 cup enchilada sauce (not salsa)
1 tablespoon chopped fresh parsley
2 tablespoons chopped cilantro
4 cups tortilla chips
1 teaspoon salt
1/2 teaspoon freshly ground black pepper
6 ounces mild Cheddar cheese, grated
    (1 1/2 cups)

In a large skillet, sauté onion, tomato, and chard in oil. Add corn, beans, and chicken and cook until heated through.

Stir in broth, enchilada sauce, parsley, and cilantro until blended. Add tortilla chips, salt, and pepper, cover, and cook, stirring occasionally, until chips begin to soften, about 5 minutes.

Transfer mixture to a 10" Dutch oven and top with cheese; with the lid covered with charcoal, heat until cheese bubbles, about 3 minutes. For conventional cooking, leave mixture in skillet; cover with cheese and heat over medium heat for about 3 minutes, until cheese bubbles.

Yield: 4 servings

BACON AND LEEK PIE

pastry for 9-inch single-crust pie
    (recipe on page 143)
2 tablespoons butter
2 cups chopped leeks
1/4 cup chopped fresh parsley
1 teaspoon unbleached all-purpose flour
6 slices uncooked bacon, cut into
    1/2-inch pieces
3 large eggs
2/3 cup whipping cream
1/3 cup milk
1/4 teaspoon salt
1/4 teaspoon pepper
1/8 teaspoon nutmeg

Prepare pie crust according to recipe or package instructions. Place crust in Dutch oven and up sides at least 1 inch, folding excess over to form double edges, or place in 9" pie dish. Pierce crust bottom all over with fork and bake until pale golden (at 350°F in conventional oven), about 10 minutes.

Melt butter in a skillet, add leeks and parsley, and sauté until soft. Stir in flour. Spoon mixture onto crust.

Cook bacon until crisp and drain. Sprinkle bacon over leeks.

In a separate bowl, beat eggs, cream, milk, salt, pepper, and nutmeg and pour into crust. Bake in Dutch oven about 25 minutes, or in 350°F conventional oven for 45 to 50 minutes, until set in center.

Yield: 6 servings

POSH POTATO AND SAUSAGE BREAKFAST

6 medium red potatoes, quartered
2 tablespoons olive oil
1 medium onion, diced
2 large scallions, sliced crosswise
1 large tomato, chopped
1 tablespoon minced fresh basil
¼ teaspoon dried oregano
⅛ teaspoon dried thyme
salt and freshly ground black pepper to
    taste
¾ pound bulk sausage
4 ounces Cheddar cheese, grated (1 cup)
4 ounces sour cream
½ teaspoon paprika

Boil the potatoes until tender.

Heat oil and sauté potatoes until lightly browned, about 10 minutes. Add onions, scallions, tomato, basil, oregano, thyme, and salt and pepper; sauté until onions are tender and set aside.

Brown sausage; drain. Toss sausage with potato mixture and transfer to Dutch oven or 2-quart casserole dish.

Bake for 5 minutes in Dutch oven, or 10 minutes in 350°F conventional oven. Sprinkle cheese on top, and bake until cheese is bubbly, about 10 minutes. Top with sour cream, sprinkle with paprika, and serve.

Yield: 4 servings

DUTCH OVEN SAUSAGE AND POTATOES

2 tablespoons plus 1 tablespoon olive oil
6 unpeeled red-skinned potatoes,
    cut into ½-inch cubes
2 medium onions, chopped
½ pound fully cooked smoked turkey
    sausage, sliced ¼-inch thick on
    the diagonal
2 tablespoons fresh thyme
    (or 1 teaspoon dried)
1½ to 2 teaspoons cumin seed, slightly
    crushed
¼ teaspoon salt
¼ teaspoon pepper

Heat 2 tablespoons of the oil in a large skillet or Dutch oven. Cook potatoes and onion, uncovered, for about 12 minutes or until potatoes are nearly tender, stirring occasionally.

Add sausage and the remaining 1 tablespoon of oil and cook, stirring often, about 10 minutes longer until potatoes and onions are tender and slightly brown. Stir in thyme, cumin, salt, and pepper.

Yield: 6 servings

CREEK BANK SPUDS

1 pound bacon, cooked and drained
    (reserve 1/8 cup of the fat)
4 potatoes, unpeeled, parboiled, and cut
    into chunks
1 1/2 onions, chopped
2 tablespoons butter, melted
salt and freshly ground black pepper to
    taste

Crumble cooked bacon. Combine potatoes, onions, and bacon with butter and reserved bacon fat. Add salt and pepper to taste. Spread across bottom of a Dutch oven or 9"x 11" casserole dish.

    Bake in Dutch oven for 20 minutes, or in 350°F conventional oven for 30 minutes.

Yield: 4 servings

FAMOUS-ON-TWO-CONTINENTS PANCAKES

John Caccia, owner of Idaho Bolo, Etc., in Ketchum, Idaho, and a seasoned river guide, adopted this pancake recipe while living in Australia. There, the pancakes are called "pikelets."

1 cup whole wheat flour
1 cup unbleached all-purpose flour
1 teaspoon baking powder
1/2 teaspoon salt
1 teaspoon ground cinnamon
1/4 to 1/3 cup brown sugar (to taste)
1/2 cup roasted sunflower seeds and/or
    raisins
dash vanilla extract
2 tablespoons vegetable oil
1 cup (or so) of one of the following:
    ginger ale, beer, milk, pineapple juice,
    coconut milk, or fruit juice
    of your choice
2 small bananas (or 1 very large), mashed
1 egg, lightly beaten (optional)

Mix wheat flour, all-purpose flour, baking powder, salt, cinnamon, brown sugar, and sunflower seeds and/or raisins. Add vanilla, vegetable oil, and chosen liquid (with egg, if desired) and stir. Stir banana(s) into batter.

    Cook on seasoned griddle. You can also use a Dutch oven lid as a griddle. Serve with your favorite toppings.

Yield: about 15 4-inch pancakes

SOURDOUGH PANCAKES

1 cup Sourdough Starter
    (recipe on page 48)
2½ cups unbleached all-purpose flour
2 cups lukewarm water
2 eggs, beaten
3 tablespoons vegetable oil
½ teaspoon salt
1½ teaspoons baking soda
¼ cup buttermilk
1 pint fresh blueberries, washed and
    drained (optional)
oil for greasing griddle

The night before, place the starter in a large glass bowl. Pour in flour and water and mix until smooth. Cover the bowl and place it in a draft-free place overnight.

When you are ready to prepare the pancakes, add the eggs, oil, salt, baking soda, and buttermilk to starter. Mix well and let rest for 10 minutes. Then add blueberries, if desired.

Lightly oil griddle. Pour batter ¼ cup at a time and cook cakes for 2 to 3 minutes, or until small bubbles form on them. Turn and cook 1 to 2 minutes longer. Serve with your favorite toppings.

Yield: about 15 4-inch pancakes

GINGERBREAD CORN CAKES

These soft, spicy hotcakes are delicious eaten with apples in any form. Top with a mound of sweetened whipped cream or yogurt cheese and a dash of nutmeg.

1 cup whole wheat flour
¼ cup unbleached all-purpose flour
¼ cup yellow cornmeal
2½ teaspoons baking powder
1 teaspoon ground ginger
½ teaspoon ground cinnamon
½ teaspoon ground cloves
½ teaspoon nutmeg
½ teaspoon salt
¼ cup molasses
1¾ cups milk
¼ cup vegetable oil
2 eggs, beaten
oil for greasing griddle

Mix whole wheat flour, all-purpose flour, cornmeal, baking powder, ginger, cinnamon, cloves, nutmeg, salt, and molasses. Make a well in the center of mixture and set aside.

Whisk the milk and oil with the beaten eggs. Pour into well in dry ingredients. Mix just until smooth. The batter will be thin to start with but will thicken as it stands. Let rest 5 minutes.

Lightly oil griddle. Pour batter ¼ cup at a time and cook cakes for 2 to 3 minutes, or until small bubbles form on them. Turn and cook 1 to 2 minutes longer.

Yield: about 10 4-inch pancakes

KLINKHAMMER COFFEE CAKE

Charlie Shepp and Peter Klinkhammer purchased Shepp Ranch on the Main Salmon River in Idaho in the early 1900s. Pete spent nearly fifty years on this ranch, selling it in 1950 for $10,000—ten times what was paid for it.

Cake:

1 ¼ cups brown sugar
2 ½ cups whole wheat flour
1 tablespoon baking powder
¼ teaspoon baking soda
¼ teaspoon salt
½ cup unsalted butter
3 eggs, lightly beaten
1 cup milk
1 teaspoon vanilla extract
1 cup plain yogurt

Topping:

¼ cup butter, melted
¾ cup chopped walnuts
¾ cup brown sugar
1 ½ teaspoons ground cinnamon
¾ cup raisins

Line Dutch oven or 9"x 11" baking pan with parchment paper, extending paper two inches up sides and set aside.

Mix brown sugar, whole wheat flour, baking powder, baking soda, and salt.

In a separate dish, melt butter, then add beaten eggs, milk, vanilla, and yogurt. Make a well in the dry ingredients and pour in the liquids. Mix only to moisten the dry ingredients. Pour batter into Dutch oven or pan.

Partially bake batter in Dutch oven for 25 minutes, or in 350°F conventional oven for 35 minutes, before adding topping.

While batter is baking, make the topping: Stir together melted butter, walnuts, brown sugar, cinnamon, and raisins.

After initial baking time, sprinkle topping mixture on top of cake and bake another 5 to 10 minutes or until a knife comes out of the center nearly clean. Cool slightly before slicing.

Yield: 10 to 12 servings

APPLE CINNAMON BROWN BETTY

This great breakfast dish can also be served as a dessert topped with whipped cream or ice cream. Try making it with peaches instead of apples.

butter for greasing pan
½ pound (2 sticks) unsalted butter, melted
2 cups rolled oats
2 cups unbleached all-purpose flour
2 cups brown sugar
2 teaspoons ground cinnamon
½ teaspoon baking powder
2 tablespoons cornstarch
5 tablespoons fresh lemon juice (about 2 large lemons)
6 cups apples, peeled and sliced

Grease a 12" Dutch oven or 9" x 13" baking pan and set aside.

Mix butter, oats, flour, brown sugar, cinnamon, and baking powder. Set aside.

In a separate large bowl, mix cornstarch and lemon juice. Add apples and toss to coat with juice mixture. Sprinkle one third of the oatmeal mixture over the bottom of Dutch oven or baking pan. Spread apple mixture in an even layer on top. Sprinkle remaining oatmeal mixture evenly over apples.

Bake in Dutch oven for about 30 minutes, or in 350°F conventional oven for about 35 to 40 minutes, until topping is light golden brown. Cut into squares and serve warm.

Yield: 12 servings

BLUEBERRY CINNAMON BROWN BETTY

This also makes a great dessert topped with ice cream. Equivalent amounts of sliced apples, peaches, or pitted cherries can be substituted for the blueberries.

butter for greasing pan
½ pound (2 sticks) unsalted butter, melted
2 cups rolled oats
2 cups unbleached all-purpose flour
2 cups brown sugar
2 teaspoons ground cinnamon
½ teaspoon baking powder
2 tablespoons cornstarch
5 tablespoons fresh lemon juice (need about 2 large lemons)
3½ pints fresh blueberries, rinsed and picked over

Grease a 12" Dutch oven or 9"x 13" baking pan and set aside.

Mix butter, oats, flour, brown sugar, cinnamon, and baking powder in large bowl and set aside.

In a separate large bowl, mix cornstarch and lemon juice. Add blueberries and toss to coat.

Sprinkle one third of the oatmeal mixture over the bottom of Dutch oven or baking pan. Spread all the blueberries in an even layer on top. Sprinkle remaining oatmeal mixture evenly over blueberries.

Bake in Dutch oven for about 30 minutes, or in 350°F conventional oven for about 35 to 40 minutes, until topping is light golden brown. Cut into squares and serve warm.

Yield: 12 servings

BLUEBERRY COBBLER

Cobblers have always been a favorite of the Dutch oven cook, and this one is exceptional. You can also serve this for dessert with a topping of vanilla ice cream.

Filling:

4 cups fresh blueberries
5 tablespoons sugar
¾ cup orange juice

Topping:

1 cup unbleached all-purpose flour
½ teaspoon baking powder
⅛ teaspoon salt
½ pound (2 sticks) butter, softened
1 cup sugar
1 egg
½ teaspoon vanilla extract

Mix blueberries, 5 tablespoons sugar, and orange juice. Pour in a 12" Dutch oven or 9"x 13" baking pan and set aside.

Make the topping: Mix the flour, baking powder, and salt in a small bowl and set aside. Mix the butter and the remaining 1 cup of sugar until well blended. Stir in egg and vanilla; then stir in flour mixture. Drop topping by the tablespoonful on top of the blueberry mixture.

Bake in Dutch oven for 30 to 40 minutes, or in 350°F conventional oven for 40 to 45 minutes, until cobbler topping is golden brown and filling is bubbly. Cool slightly before serving.

Yield: 8 to 10 servings

SINFUL STICKY BUNS

The seductive flavors of caramel and sweet butter and the crunch of nuts makes these buns the highlight of any breakfast or brunch.

Buns:

2 packages active dry yeast
1/2 cup warm water
2 cups warm milk
1/2 cup vegetable shortening
6 tablespoons sugar
2 teaspoons salt
2 eggs
6 1/2 cups unbleached all-purpose flour

Caramel Glaze:

1 cup (2 sticks) unsalted butter
3 cups brown sugar
1/2 cup light corn syrup
3 cups broken pecan or walnut pieces

Dissolve the yeast in the warm water.

In a large bowl, mix milk, shortening, sugar, salt, and eggs until well blended. Add the yeast and 4 cups of the flour; mix vigorously. Add the rest of the flour to make a soft dough. Knead for 1 minute. Let dough rest for 10 minutes, then knead again until the dough is smooth and elastic. Cover it and let rise until it doubles in bulk.

Make the caramel glaze: Put butter, brown sugar, and corn syrup in a saucepan. Heat and stir until the butter is melted and the sugar dissolved. Remove from heat and pour 1 cup of glaze into a small bowl and set aside. Sprinkle the remaining glaze over the bottom of a 12" Dutch oven or 9"x 12" baking pan and sprinkle nuts over the glaze.

Roll out the dough into a rectangle and spread with glaze. Roll up like a jelly roll from the wide side into a long tube. Cut into 1 1/2-inch pieces. Place each piece in the Dutch oven, flat side down. Cover and let rise until puffy.

Bake in Dutch oven for 25 to 30 minutes, or in 350°F conventional oven for 30 to 35 minutes. Invert pan onto waxed paper. Serve warm.

Yield: 12 large buns

APPLESAUCE OATMEAL MUFFINS

Applesauce adds extra moistness to these whole-grain muffins.

Muffins:

1 ½ cups rolled oats
1 ¼ cups unbleached all-purpose flour
¾ teaspoon ground cinnamon
1 tablespoon baking powder
¾ tablespoon baking soda
1 cup unsweetened applesauce
½ cup skim milk
½ cup brown sugar
3 tablespoons vegetable oil
1 egg white

Topping:

¼ cup oats
1 tablespoon brown sugar
¼ teaspoon ground cinnamon
1 tablespoon butter, melted

Line 12 medium-sized muffin cups with paper baking cups, or line bottom of Dutch oven with 12 paper muffin cups.

Combine oats, flour, ¾ teaspoon cinnamon, baking powder, and baking soda in a large bowl. Blend in applesauce, skim milk, ½ cup brown sugar, vegetable oil, and egg white, and mix until dry ingredients are moistened. Fill muffin cups two-thirds full.

Make the topping: Combine oats, 1 tablespoon brown sugar, ¼ teaspoon cinnamon, and butter. Sprinkle over batter.

Bake muffins in Dutch oven for 20 minutes, or in 400°F conventional oven for 20 minutes, or until deep golden brown.

Yield: about 1 dozen

BREADS

REMEMBER

When a recipe calls for baking, braising, stewing, or roasting, the Dutch oven must be covered with charcoal briquettes on top of the lid. For boiling, frying, sautéing, and quick-heating, leave the Dutch oven cover off. For more on cooking techniques for the Dutch oven, see "Dutch Oven Care and Use," pages 2–3.

CORN BREAD

butter for greasing pan
1¾ cup yellow cornmeal
¼ cup whole wheat flour
¼ cup powdered milk
3 tablespoons baking powder
1 teaspoon sea salt
1 egg, lightly beaten
1 tablespoon honey
2 tablespoons butter
1½ cups milk

Butter a Dutch oven or 9"x 9" baking pan.

Combine cornmeal, flour, powdered milk, baking powder, and salt. Add egg, honey, butter, and milk, and stir until moist. Pour batter into Dutch oven or pan.

Bake in Dutch oven for 20 minutes, or in 425°F conventional oven for 20 to 25 minutes.

Yield: 6 servings

SOUR CREAM BUTTERMILK CORN BREAD

butter for greasing pan
2 cups white cornmeal
3½ teaspoons baking powder
½ teaspoon baking soda
dash salt
1½ cups low-fat sour cream
2 eggs, lightly beaten
2 tablespoons olive oil
⅔ cup buttermilk

Butter a 12" Dutch oven or 9"x 12" baking pan.

Combine cornmeal, baking powder, baking soda, and salt.

In a separate bowl, lightly beat together sour cream, eggs, olive oil, and buttermilk. Combine gently with the dry ingredients; do not overmix. Pour batter into Dutch oven or pan.

Bake for 30 minutes in Dutch oven, or 30 to 35 minutes in 375°F conventional oven, until lightly browned. This is delicious served with Saucy Chicken (recipe on page 76).

Yield: 6 servings

NO-KNEAD OATMEAL BREAD

butter for greasing pans and rising bowl
2 cups boiling water
1 cup rolled oats
⅓ cup vegetable shortening
½ cup light molasses (or honey)
1 tablespoon salt
2 packages active dry yeast
2 eggs, lightly beaten
6½ cups whole wheat flour
flour for rolling out dough

Butter a bowl *or* two Dutch ovens; if cooking conventionally, butter a bowl *and* two loaf pans.

Combine boiling water, oats, shortening, molasses or honey, and salt. Cool to lukewarm. Add yeast and mix well. Blend in eggs. Gradually add flour, mixing until dough is well blended. Place dough in greased bowl or Dutch oven and cover; let rise until double. (If you want to bake the dough later in the day, you may put it in a refrigerator or cold place for several hours.)

Shape dough into two loaves on a well-floured board and place in two loaf pans covered with damp towels or plastic wrap, or in two covered Dutch ovens. Let rise in warm place until doubled in bulk, about 2 hours.

Bake in Dutch oven for 45 minutes, or in a 350°F conventional oven for 1 hour.

Yield: 2 loaves

OATMEAL BUTTERMILK BREAD

1 cup, plus 1 tablespoon quick-cooking
  oats
1 ½ cups unbleached all-purpose flour
½ cup whole wheat flour
1 teaspoon baking powder
½ teaspoon baking soda
½ teaspoon salt
1 cup buttermilk
¼ cup canola oil
¼ cup molasses
1 egg

Line a 10" Dutch oven or 9"x 12" baking pan with parchment paper, extending the paper two inches up sides.

Toast 1 cup of oats in separate Dutch oven for about 15 minutes, or toast on baking sheet in 450°F conventional oven for ten minutes. Combine toasted oats, all-purpose flour, wheat flour, baking powder, baking soda, and salt, and stir well. Make a well in center of mixture.

In a separate bowl, combine buttermilk, oil, molasses, and egg. Pour into dry ingredients and stir just until moistened. Spoon batter into Dutch oven or pan. Sprinkle with the remaining oats.

Bake for 40 to 50 minutes in Dutch oven, or 35 to 40 minutes in 350°F conventional oven, or until a toothpick inserted in the center comes out clean.

Yield: 8 servings

BANANA-CARROT BREAD

butter for greasing pan
1 cup whole wheat flour
1 cup unbleached all-purpose flour
1 teaspoon baking powder
1 teaspoon baking soda
½ teaspoon ground cinnamon
¼ teaspoon salt
⅛ teaspoon ground cloves
¼ cup margarine
¾ cup brown sugar
3 eggs, lightly beaten
2 large, very ripe bananas, peeled
    and mashed
1¼ teaspoons vanilla extract
2 large carrots, finely grated
½ cup chopped walnuts

Butter a 12" Dutch oven or loaf pan.

In a large bowl, combine flours, baking powder, baking soda, cinnamon, salt, and cloves and set aside.

In a medium bowl, cream margarine and brown sugar. Beat in eggs, bananas, and vanilla. Add banana mixture to dry ingredients until just blended. Stir in carrots and walnuts. Pour into Dutch oven or pan.

Bake for 1 hour in Dutch oven, or 55 to 60 minutes in 350°F conventional oven, or until a knife inserted in the center of the loaf comes out clean.

Yield: 1 loaf

BIG BEND BANANA-WALNUT BREAD

1 cup unbleached all-purpose flour
1 cup whole wheat flour
1 cup brown sugar
1 tablespoon baking powder
1 teaspoon ground cinnamon
¼ teaspoon baking soda
4 egg whites
1 cup mashed bananas
½ cup buttermilk
⅓ cup applesauce
1 teaspoon vanilla extract
½ cup chopped walnuts

Line a 12" Dutch oven or loaf pan with parchment paper, extending the paper two inches up sides.

In a large bowl, combine all-purpose flour, wheat flour, brown sugar, baking powder, cinnamon, and baking soda and set aside.

Beat egg whites until foamy. Add bananas, buttermilk, applesauce, and vanilla. Stir into dry ingredients until just blended. Add nuts. Pour into Dutch oven or pan.

Bake in Dutch oven for 45 to 55 minutes, or in 375°F conventional oven for 45 minutes, or until golden.

Yield: 12 servings

ZUCCHINI BREAD

butter for greasing pan
flour for dusting pan
3 cups whole wheat flour
I teaspoon salt
I teaspoon ground cinnamon
I teaspoon ginger
I teaspoon baking soda
¼ teaspoon baking powder
I cup chopped walnuts
3 eggs
I cup honey
I cup vegetable oil
3 teaspoons vanilla
2 cups washed and grated zucchini
        (unpeeled)

Butter and flour two 10" Dutch ovens or two loaf pans.

In a large bowl, mix flour, salt, cinnamon, ginger, baking soda, baking powder, and walnuts.

In a separate bowl, mix eggs, honey, and oil. Blend in vanilla and grated zucchini. Mix wet ingredients into dry. Pour batter into Dutch ovens or loaf pans.

Bake in Dutch ovens for about 1 hour, turning oven every 15 minutes, or in a 325°F conventional oven for 1 hour. Bread is done when a knife inserted in its center comes out clean. Remove from pan and let cool before slicing.

Yield: 2 loaves

BRAN WHEAT MUFFINS

I cup unbleached all-purpose flour
I cup whole wheat flour
¾ cup whole bran cereal
3 teaspoons baking powder
½ teaspoon salt
I egg
¼ cup oil or butter, melted
4 tablespoons honey
I cup milk
butter for greasing muffin cups, unless
        using paper liners

Mix all-purpose flour, wheat flour, cereal, baking powder, and salt. Form a well in the center of the mixture.

In a separate bowl, lightly beat the egg and stir in butter or oil, honey, and milk. Pour all at once into the well of the flour mixture. Stir to just moisten ingredients, scraping the bottom of the bowl as you stir. Batter should look lumpy.

Grease cups of one 12-muffin tin or line them with paper baking cups or, if using a Dutch oven, line the bottom with twelve paper baking cups. Fill each muffin cup two-thirds full with batter.

Bake in Dutch oven for 15 to 20 minutes, or in a 375°F conventional oven for about 25 minutes, or until well browned. Serve muffins hot with butter or honey.

Yield: 1 dozen

ANGIE'S CHEESE CRACKERS

My sister-in-law, Angie Mills, shared this recipe with me.

butter for greasing pan
1 cup unbleached all-purpose flour
1/4 teaspoon baking soda
1/2 teaspoon salt
1/2 cup cornmeal
1/4 cup wheat germ
1/2 cup butter
2 ounces Cheddar cheese, grated (1/2 cup)
1/4 cup milk
1 tablespoon vinegar

Liberally grease a Dutch oven or baking sheet and set aside.

Combine all other ingredients. Roll dough out to about 1/4-inch thickness and pat into bottom of Dutch oven or onto baking sheet. Score lines with a fork for breaking.

Bake in Dutch oven for 15 to 20 minutes, or in 400°F conventional oven for 15 to 20 minutes, until golden brown. Cool and break along scored lines.

Yield: 12 crackers

PARMESAN PUFFS

These savory puffs are great as appetizers or served with soup.

butter for greasing pan
1/4 cup milk
1/4 cup water
1/4 cup unsalted butter
1/4 teaspoon salt
1/2 cup unbleached all-purpose flour
2 large eggs
4 ounces Parmesan cheese, grated (1 cup)
freshly ground black pepper to taste

Butter a Dutch oven or baking sheet.

Combine milk, water, butter, and salt in a saucepan and bring to a boil. Reduce the heat and add flour. Beat the mixture until it leaves the side of the pan and forms a ball. Transfer the mixture to a bowl. Whisk in the eggs, one at a time, whisking well after each addition. Stir in Parmesan and pepper.

Drop the batter in eight mounds in Dutch oven or baking pan. Bake the puffs in Dutch oven with a lot of coals on the top, or in 400°F conventional oven, for about 20 minutes, or until they are crisp and golden.

Yield: 12 puffs

RICOTTA PUFFS

1 cup low-fat ricotta cheese
3 eggs
¼ cup sugar
1 cup unbleached all-purpose flour
4 teaspoons baking powder
¼ teaspoon salt
24 ounces peanut or canola oil for frying
2 cups confectioner's sugar

Beat ricotta cheese, eggs, and sugar until blended and smooth.

In a separate bowl, blend flour, baking powder, and salt. Beat into cheese to form a smooth, thick batter.

Heat oil in Dutch oven or large kettle. Drop batter by the teaspoonful in the oil, frying several at a time. Fry puffs until golden brown on all sides. Drain well. Dust with confectioner's sugar and serve warm.

Yield: about 3 dozen puffs

PARMESAN POPOVERS

5 egg whites
1⅓ cups milk
3 tablespoons butter, melted
1⅓ cups unbleached all-purpose flour
1½ teaspoons mixed dried herbs such as basil, oregano, and parsley
3 tablespoons grated Parmesan cheese
butter for greasing muffin cups

Mix egg whites, milk, and butter in a large bowl. Stir in flour, herbs, and Parmesan until just combined. Let batter rest for 5 minutes.

Grease a popover or muffin tin, or line Dutch oven with paper muffin cups. Spoon batter into each cup, filling each two-thirds full.

Bake in Dutch oven for 15 minutes. For conventional cooking, bake in 450°F oven for 12 to 15 minutes, reduce heat to 350°F, and bake until popovers are firm and golden brown, 10 to 12 minutes longer. Serve immediately.

Yield: 12 popovers

FOCACCIA FLATS

Frozen bread dough makes a quick loaf of flat bread, similar to Italian focaccia. Use for pizza-like hot prosciutto-and-cheese open-faced sandwiches.

butter for greasing pan
flour for rolling out dough
1 loaf frozen bread dough, thawed
¼ cup olive oil
1 teaspoon coarse salt
¼ pound prosciutto, thinly sliced
8 ounces mozzarella cheese, grated
    (2 cups)
1 tablespoon red wine vinegar
⅛ teaspoon crushed dried hot red chiles
⅓ cup finely chopped red onion
2 tablespoons drained capers

Butter a 12" Dutch oven, or butter a 12-inch circle on a baking sheet. Roll bread dough out into a 12" circle on a floured table, and ease dough into Dutch oven or onto baking sheet. With fingers, poke deep holes in dough at 2-inch intervals. Brush with 2 tablespoons of the olive oil and sprinkle with coarse salt. Cover and let rise until doubled.

Bake in Dutch oven for 12 to 15 minutes, or in 350°F conventional oven for 20 to 25 minutes, until golden brown. Cover focaccia with prosciutto and cheese.

Stir together remaining oil, vinegar, chiles, onion, and capers. Spoon onion mixture evenly over cheese. Return lid and bake until cheese melts and is lightly browned. Cut into wedges and serve hot.

Yield: 4 to 6 servings

BAKED CINNAMON SCONES

butter for greasing pans
2 cups whole wheat flour
1 tablespoon baking powder
1 teaspoon baking soda
1 tablespoon sugar
1/2 teaspoon salt
1/2 teaspoon cinnamon
2 tablespoons oil
1/2 cup buttermilk

Butter a Dutch oven or two baking sheets.

Combine flour, baking powder, baking soda, sugar, salt, and cinnamon in a large bowl. Stir in oil and milk with a fork until mixture clings to itself. Knead dough gently for 3 minutes.

Divide dough into three parts. Roll out each part to 1/2-inch thick. Cut into six wedges or use a small glass or cutter to cut into 2-inch rounds. Place in Dutch oven or on baking sheets.

Bake in a Dutch oven for 10 to 15 minutes, or in a 450° conventional oven for 10 to 15 minutes. Serve hot.

Yield: 18 scones

CURRANT SCONES

3 cups unbleached all-purpose flour
3 tablespoons sugar
1 teaspoon baking soda
1/2 teaspoon salt
6 tablespoons chilled unsalted butter
1/3 cup dried currants
1 egg, lightly beaten
3/4 cup plus 3 tablespoons buttermilk
flour for rolling out dough
1 tablespoon milk

Line a 12" Dutch oven or baking sheet with parchment paper. If using a conventional oven, preheat oven to 375°F.

Mix flour, sugar, baking soda, and salt in a large bowl. Cut in butter until mixture is like coarse cornmeal. Mix in currants. Mix in egg and buttermilk to form a soft dough.

Turn dough out onto a floured surface. Pat dough into a 3/4-inch-thick round. Cut out rounds with a 2½-inch cutter or glass, using all the dough. Put into Dutch oven or on baking sheet and brush tops with milk.

Bake in Dutch oven for about 18 minutes, or in 375°F conventional oven for 20 minutes, until scones are golden brown. Serve warm with butter and jam.

Yield: 15 scones

SWEET POTATO PECAN MUFFINS

These are great low-calorie muffins. Serve with soups or salads.

1 medium-sized sweet potato
margarine for greasing muffin tins
½ cup skim milk
½ teaspoon lemon juice
½ cup oats
½ cupshredded wheat bran cereal
⅓ cup dark brown sugar
¼ cup vegetable oil
1 egg
⅔ cup unbleached all-purpose flour
½ teaspoon baking powder
¼ teaspoon baking soda
¼ teaspoon salt
½ teaspoon ground cinnamon
3 teaspoons chopped pecans

Bake sweet potato in Dutch oven, conventional oven, or microwave; cool until it can be handled easily. Peel and mash the potato. Set aside ⅓ cup potato; reserve rest for another use.

Grease 12 muffin tins or use paper muffin cups.

In a separate bowl, combine milk, lemon juice, oats, and cereal. Stir well. Add mashed potato, brown sugar, oil, and egg. Beat until smooth and set aside.

In a large bowl, combine flour, baking powder, baking soda, salt, and cinnamon. Make a well in the center of the dry ingredients and pour in oat mixture. Stir just until ingredients are moistened.

Spoon 3 tablespoons batter into each of twelve muffin cups or paper muffin cups inside Dutch oven. Sprinkle each muffin with ¼ teaspoon chopped pecans.

Bake in Dutch oven for 15 minutes, or in 375°F conventional oven for 15 minutes.

Yield: 12 muffins

WHOLE WHEAT BREAD

butter for greasing pans and rising bowl
4 packages active dry yeast
3½ cups warm water
I cup honey
3 tablespoons oil
I teaspoon salt
9 cups whole wheat flour
flour for rolling out dough

Liberally butter a bowl and two Dutch ovens; if cooking conventionally, liberally butter a bowl and three loaf pans.

Dissolve yeast in warm water in a large bowl. Add honey and stir until dissolved. Add oil and salt and stir well. Add flour one cup at a time, mixing until you have a stiff dough.

Turn dough out onto floured surface and knead until smooth and elastic, about 5 minutes. Shape dough into a ball. Place the dough in oiled bowl and cover with a damp towel or plastic wrap. Let rise until double in size, or about 2 hours.

Cut the dough into two portions for two Dutch ovens or three portions for loaf pans. Shape dough into round or oblong loaves, depending on shape of pans, and place in Dutch ovens or pans. Let rise until double in size.

Bake loaves in Dutch oven for 25 to 30 minutes, or in 350°F conventional oven for about 35 to 40 minutes, until golden brown. Remove from pans immediately and cool slightly before slicing.

Yield: 2 to 3 loaves

OATMEAL BREAD

This moist bread tastes wonderful and keeps well.

butter for greasing pans and rising bowl
¾ cup milk
I package active dry yeast
I cup quick oats
I¼ cups boiling water
I½ teaspoons salt
½ cup dark molasses
I tablespoon unsalted butter
5 cups unbleached all-purpose flour

Butter a bowl and two loaf pans or a bowl and two Dutch ovens.

Heat milk over medium heat until a skim forms on the surface. Cool to lukewarm, then stir in yeast. Set aside.

Stir boiling water, salt, and molasses into oats. Cool mixture to lukewarm, then blend in butter, flour, and milk-yeast mixture. Mix until you have a soft dough. Place dough in oiled bowl and cover with a damp towel or plastic wrap. Let dough rise in a warm place until doubled.

Knead lightly about 3 minutes. Shape into two loaves and place in loaf pans or Dutch ovens. Let rise until double again. Bake in Dutch oven for 45 to 50 minutes, or in 350°F for about 1 hour.

Yield: 2 loaves

WHITE CREEK WALNUT BREAD

Note that some food-processing will need to be done ahead for this recipe.

3 cups plus 2 cups walnuts
1 cup plus 3 cups unbleached all-purpose
    flour
oil for greasing rising bowl
½ cup warm water
1 tablespoon molasses
1 tablespoon active dry yeast
2 cups milk, at room temperature
3 cups whole wheat flour
1½ teaspoon salt
¼ teaspoon nutmeg
1 tablespoon soy sauce
2 tablespoons walnut oil
2 eggs
2 tablespoons milk

Do ahead: Grind 3 cups of the walnuts with 1 cup of the all-purpose flour in a blender or food processor until very fine.

Line a 12" Dutch oven or loaf pan with parchment paper, extending paper two inches up sides. Oil bowl for rising.

In a small bowl, combine warm water, molasses, and yeast. Set aside in a warm place until yeast dissolves. Add milk to yeast mixture, then beat in whole wheat flour. Place in oiled bowl and cover with a damp towel or plastic wrap. Let dough rise 1 hour.

Stir dough, and then beat in salt, nutmeg, soy sauce, walnut oil, and one egg.

Add ground walnut–flour mixture to bread dough. Then stir in enough all-purpose flour to make a dough that pulls away from the sides of the bowl. Cover and let sit for 10 minutes.

Knead in the remainder of the all-purpose flour to make a smooth, soft, and slightly sticky dough. Let rise, covered, for 1 hour until dough doubles in size.

While bread is rising, chop the remaining 2 cups of walnuts and toast for 10 minutes in a Dutch oven or in 350°F conventional oven. Beat the remaining egg with 2 tablespoons milk.

Punch down the dough and knead in toasted walnuts. Place in Dutch oven or pan and let rise for about 30 minutes. Glaze loaf with egg-milk mixture.

Bake in Dutch oven for 45 to 55 minutes, or in 375°F conventional oven for 50 to 60 minutes, until loaf is brown and sounds hollow when tapped.

Yield: 1 loaf

PARROT PLACER POPPY-SEED BREAD

This bread is named for Earl Parrot, a hermit who lived in Impassable Canyon, on the Middle Fork of the Salmon River, from 1917 until 1942. He had a beautiful garden near his cabin, which was only accessible by a 2,000-foot ascent to the canyon rim. In 1990 there remained at the site only the remnants of rhubarb plants, a few fruit trees, and irrigation ditches.

6 cups unbleached all-purpose flour
¾ cup whole wheat flour
I cup rye flour
½ cup poppy seeds
1½ tablespoons sea salt
I teaspoon fast-acting yeast
2¾ cups warm water
oil for greasing rising bowl
cornmeal for dusting pan
cold water
2 tablespoons poppy seeds

Combine all-purpose flour, wheat flour, rye flour, poppy seeds, sea salt, yeast, and warm water. (If you are doing this at home, you may use a mixer or food processor with a dough hook attachment.) Knead 10 to 15 minutes if doing by hand and 5 minutes if using a mixer or food processor. Add more warm water if needed, until you have a smooth, elastic dough. Cover with plastic wrap or towel and let rise in oiled bowl or Dutch oven in warm place for the afternoon (or 12 hours in your kitchen).

Dust two Dutch ovens or two loaf pans with cornmeal.

Divide dough in half and form two round loaves. Brush the tops of the loaves with cold water and sprinkle with poppy seeds. Place loaves, poppy seed side up, into Dutch ovens or pans. Let the loaves rise until they have doubled in size.

Bake in Dutch oven for 35 to 40 minutes, or in 350°F conventional oven for 45 to 50 minutes, until crusts are golden brown.

Yield: 2 loaves

PARMESAN BREAD

This is a delicious bread to serve with salads.

4 packages active dry yeast
4 teaspoon sugar
¼ cup warm water
8 ounces Parmesan cheese, grated
  (2 cups)
3½ cups plus 3 cups unbleached
  all-purpose flour
2 teaspoons salt
6 eggs, beaten lightly
1½ cups unsalted butter, melted and
  cooled
oil for coating loaves
butter for greasing pans

Dissolve yeast and sugar in warm water. In a spearate bowl, mix together Parmesan, 3½ cups of the flour, and salt. Beat in the yeast and eggs; beat mixture for 3 minutes. Add butter and continue beating the mixture, adding the remaining flour as needed to keep the dough from sticking. Knead until a smooth and silky dough is formed. Coat it with oil, cover, and let rise in a covered bowl in a warm place for 2 hours.

Butter three loaf pans or two Dutch ovens.

Cut the dough into two portions for two Dutch ovens or three portions for loaf pans. Shape dough into round or oblong loaves, depending on shape of pans, and place in Dutch ovens or pans. Let rise until double in size.

Bake in Dutch ovens for 25 to 30 minutes, or in 350°F conventional oven for 30 to 35 minutes, until loaves are pale golden and sound hollow when tapped.

Yield: 2 to 3 loaves

SAGE AND OLIVE FOCACCIA BREAD

Focaccia, a mouth-watering Italian delight, is simpler to make than pizza, because it is usually topped with just a coating of olive oil and a sprinkling of spices and/or herbs. Serve as a snack or a bread.

oil for greasing rising bowl and pan
2 packages active dry yeast
1½ cups lukewarm water
3½ to 4 cups unbleached all-purpose
　　flour
1 cup rye flour
1 tablespoon sage
2 teaspoons rosemary
¼ cup chopped Kalamata olives
2 tablespoons olive oil

Grease a 12" Dutch oven or baking sheet with olive oil. Oil a bowl for rising, and set aside.

Dissolve yeast in water. Add all-purpose flour, rye flour, sage, rosemary, and olives and knead about 5 minutes, gradually working in the rest of the flour. Put dough in oiled bowl, cover with a damp towel or plastic wrap, and let double in size.

Press dough into bottom of Dutch oven or in ½-inch-thick rectangle on baking sheet, cover, and let rise until doubled in size.

Brush top of dough with remaining 2 tablespoons olive oil. Put about ten coals beneath the Dutch oven and a double layer covering the top.

Bake in Dutch oven for 10 minutes, or in 375°F conventional oven for 15 minutes, or until brown on top and pulled away from the edges of the pan.

Yield: 1 loaf

BUBBLE BREAD

oil for greasing rising bowl and pan
    (conventional cooking)
2 packages active dry yeast
1 teaspoon sugar
1 cup warm water
1 cup sliced ripe banana
$\frac{1}{2}$ cup plus 2 tablespoons pineapple-
    orange-banana juice concentrate,
    undiluted
$\frac{1}{4}$ cup honey
2 tablespoons margarine, melted
5$\frac{1}{4}$ cups unbleached all-purpose flour
1 teaspoon salt
$\frac{1}{4}$ cup cream of coconut
$\frac{1}{2}$ cup confectioner's sugar

Line Dutch oven with parchment paper, extending paper two inches up sides. If making in conventional oven, grease a 10" tube pan. Oil a bowl for rising.

Dissolve yeast and sugar in warm water and let stand 5 minutes. In a separate bowl, combine banana, $\frac{1}{2}$ cup of juice concentrate, honey, and margarine, and beat well in a blender or by hand until smooth. Set aside.

In a separate large bowl, combine 2 cups of the flour and salt and stir well. Add yeast mixture and banana mixture, stirring until well blended. Add 2$\frac{3}{4}$ more cups of the flour, stirring to form a soft dough. Knead until smooth and elastic, adding remaining flour as needed to prevent dough from sticking to hands. Place in oiled bowl, cover with a damp towel or plastic wrap, and let rise until doubled in size.

Punch down dough and form about thirty 1$\frac{1}{2}$–inch balls. Layer balls in Dutch oven or tube pan.

In a small bowl, combine cream of coconut and remaining 2 tablespoons juice concentrate and stir well. Pour 3 tablespoons of juice mixture over dough. Cover dough and let rise until doubled again.

Bake in Dutch oven for 30 minutes, or in 350°F conventional oven for 30 minutes, or until loaf sounds hollow when tapped. Stir confectioner's sugar into remaining juice mixture and drizzle over top of warm bread.

Yield: 1 loaf

SOURDOUGH WHOLE WHEAT BREAD

Sourdough Starter:

1 package active dry yeast
½ cup warm water
2 cups lukewarm water
2 cups unbleached all-purpose flour
1 teaspoon salt
1 tablespoon sugar

Bread Dough:

1 package active dry yeast
1½ cups warm water
1 cup Sourdough Starter
2 teaspoons salt
2 teaspoons sugar or honey
3 cups plus 2 to 2¼ cups whole wheat
    flour
½ teaspoon baking soda
flour for rolling out dough
butter for greasing pans
melted butter for brushing on loaves

Make Sourdough Starter: Dissolve yeast in warm water. Stir in lukewarm water, flour, salt, and sugar. Beat until smooth. Let stand, uncovered at room temperature, for three to five days. Stir two or three times daily; cover at night. (Starter should have a "yeasty, " not sour, smell.) Cover, and refrigerate until ready to make bread.

To keep starter: Add ½ cup water, ½ cup flour, and 1 teaspoon sugar to leftover starter. Let stand until bubbly and well fermented, at least one day. Store in the refrigerator or cooler. If not used within ten days, add 1 teaspoon sugar.

Yield: about 3 cups

To make Sourdough Whole Wheat Bread: Soften yeast in warm water in a large bowl. Blend in Sourdough Starter batter, salt, and sugar or honey. Add 3 cups of the flour. Beat 3 to 4 minutes. Cover with a damp towel or plastic wrap and let rise until double in size (about 2 hours).

In a separate bowl, mix baking soda with 1½ cups of the flour. Stir into risen dough. Add enough additional flour to make a stiff dough. Turn dough out onto a lightly floured surface and knead for 8 to 10 minutes. Divide dough in half, cover, and let rest 10 minutes.

Lightly grease two baking sheets or two Dutch ovens and set aside.

Shape dough into two round or oval loaves. Place loaves on baking sheets or in Dutch ovens. With sharp knife, make diagonal gashes across top. Let rise until double in size (about 1½ hours).

Bake in Dutch oven for 30 to 35 minutes, or in 400°F conventional oven for 35 to 40 minutes. Brush with melted butter.

Yield: 2 loaves

ELVERA'S SOURDOUGH RYE BREAD

My friend Elvera Klein, author of Creative Sourdough Recipes, *has generously shared some of her wonderful recipes with me.*

1 cup Sourdough Starter (use recipe on page 48 or your own sourdough starter)

2 cups warm water (about 110°F)

4 cups plus 2½ to 3½ cups unbleached all-purpose flour

2 cups rye flour

2 tablespoons light molasses

2 teaspoons salt

1 teaspoon baking soda

1 tablespoon caraway seed

flour for rolling out dough

vegetable shortening for greasing rising bowl

cornmeal for dusting pans

½ cup water

1 teaspoon egg white

Prepare Sourdough Starter and set in a warm place overnight. The next morning, alternately add warm water and 4 cups of the all-purpose flour to starter. Beat well and set in warm place for about 3 hours or until bubbly.

Add to starter mixture the rye flour, molasses, salt, soda, caraway seed, and enough all-purpose flour to form a stiff dough. Turn dough out onto a lightly floured board and knead until smooth and elastic. Place dough in a greased bowl and turn dough to grease top as well. Cover with a damp towel or plastic wrap and let rise in a warm place until doubled in bulk.

Dust a baking sheet or two Dutch ovens with cornmeal. If making in conventional oven, preheat oven to 400°F.

In a small bowl mix water and egg white. Set aside.

Punch dough down and let rest about 10 minutes. Divide dough in half and knead each piece gently until smooth. Shape each piece into an oblong or round loaf. Place on baking sheet or in Dutch ovens. Set in a warm place to rise until almost double in size.

If making in conventional oven, just before baking place a pan with about ¼ inch of boiling water on the lower rack of the oven.

Cut slashes on top of loaves with a sharp knife or razor blade. Brush loaves with water–egg white mixture. Bake in Dutch oven or conventional oven about 25 to 30 minutes or until brown, brushing with water–egg white mixture again about 10 minutes before removing bread from oven. Remove from oven or coals and place on rack to cool.

Yield: 2 loaves

ELVERA'S SOURDOUGH CORN BREAD

butter for greasing pan
1½ cups yellow cornmeal
½ cup sugar
½ teaspoon salt
¾ teaspoon baking soda
1 cup Sourdough Starter (use recipe on
    page 48 or your own sourdough
    starter)
1½ cups evaporated milk or half and half
2 eggs, beaten
¼ cup butter, melted

Grease a 12" Dutch oven or 9"x 9" baking pan and set aside.

Mix cornmeal, sugar, salt, and baking soda together in a large bowl and set aside.

In a separate bowl, beat starter, milk, eggs, and butter until just mixed. Stir into cornmeal mixture until well blended.

Pour batter into Dutch oven or baking pan. Bake in Dutch oven or in 400°F oven for 25 to 30 minutes, or until a toothpick inserted in the center comes out clean. Serve hot.

Yield: 1 loaf

COTTAGE CHEESE SOURDOUGH BREAD

Rosemary Parkinson and Peggy Roskelley of Smithfield, Utah, shared their award-winning recipe from the 1988 World Championship Dutch Oven Cookoff. It is held annually in Logan, Utah, as a major event of the Festival of the American West.

1 tablespoon active dry yeast
2 cups lukewarm water
¾ cup Sourdough Starter (use recipe on page **48** or your own sourdough starter)
1 cup creamed cottage cheese
2 ounces sharp Cheddar or Longhorn cheese, grated (½ cup)
1 tablespoon chopped fresh dill
2 tablespoons chopped onion
1 tablespoon vegetable oil or melted shortening
1 tablespoon sugar
1 tablespoon salt
3 to 4 cups unbleached all-purpose flour
flour for rolling out dough
oil or melted shortening for greasing rising bowl and pan

Dissolve yeast in water. In a separate large bowl, measure sourdough starter and add cottage cheese, sharp cheese, dill, onion, oil, sugar, and salt. Add dissolved yeast. Gradually beat in enough flour, ½ cup at a time, to make a stiff dough. Reserve ½ cup flour to work into dough during kneading.

Oil a bowl for rising. Grease 14" Dutch oven or large bread pan and set aside.

Turn dough out onto a lightly floured surface and knead for 5 to 10 minutes, adding reserved flour if necessary. Put dough in oiled bowl, turning once to grease top. Cover with a damp cloth or plastic wrap. Set bowl in a warm place and let rise for 2 hours or until doubled in size. It will rise quickly on a warm day. It is wise to have the coals almost ready when the bread is ready to rise.

Place dough in bottom of Dutch oven or pan. Bake in Dutch oven with about twelve coals on the bottom and eighteen on top for about 35 minutes; or bake in 350°F conventional oven for 35 to 40 minutes.

Yield: 1 large loaf

SHERI'S BREADSTICKS

Sheri Johnson has worked for the Forest Service on the Middle Fork of the Salmon for years. During the summers she was stationed at the launch site in her trailer and prepared these great breadsticks for our guides as a special treat. This dough also makes good pizza crusts.

2½ cups water
1 tablespoon sugar
1 tablespoon salt
1 tablespoon vegetable oil
2 packages active dry yeast
7 to 7¼ cups flour (can use half whole wheat and half all-purpose)
butter for greasing pan
2 tablespoons butter, melted
¼ cup sesame seeds or poppy seeds
seasoned salt or garlic to taste

Heat water, sugar, salt, and oil until warm. Add yeast, making sure the mixture is not hot enough to kill the yeast, and stir. Add flour, and knead resulting dough until smooth and elastic. Let dough rest for 10 minutes.

Lightly grease Dutch oven or baking sheet and set aside.

Roll dough out in long rope and divide into twenty-four shorter pieces. Roll each small piece into desired breadstick shape and place on baking sheet or in Dutch oven. Brush with butter and sprinkle with sesame seeds, poppy seeds, salt, or garlic. Let rise 15 minutes.

Bake in Dutch oven for 15 minutes, or in 400°F conventional oven (on upper rack) for 15 minutes.

Yield: 48 sticks

DUTCH OVEN CINNAMON ROLLS

Whole Wheat Bread Dough:

oil for greasing rising bowl
4 packages active dry yeast
3½ cups warm water
1 cup honey
3 tablespoons oil
1 teaspoon salt
9 cups whole wheat flour

Cinnamon Rolls:

flour for rolling out dough
2 tablespoons butter, melted
½ pound (2 sticks) butter
¼ cup plus ½ cup brown sugar
1 cup raisins
½ cup chopped walnuts
1 teaspoon ground cinnamon

Oil a bowl for rising, and set aside.

Dissolve yeast in warm water in a large bowl. Add honey and stir until dissolved. Add oil and salt and stir well. Add flour one cup at a time, mixing until you have a stiff dough.

Turn dough out onto floured surface and knead until smooth and elastic, about 5 minutes. Shape dough into a ball. Place the dough in oiled bowl and cover with a damp towel or plastic wrap. Let rise for about 2 hours, until doubled in size.

Divide risen dough in half. On lightly floured board, roll out each half into a ¼-inch thick rectangle. Brush each rectangle with 1 tablespoon of the melted butter.

Melt the two sticks of butter in the bottom of a 9"x 12" baking pan or two Dutch ovens. Sprinkle with ¼ cup brown sugar (⅛ cup in each Dutch oven).

In a separate bowl, combine raisins, ½ cup brown sugar, walnuts, and cinnamon. Sprinkle half of mixture over each piece of dough. Roll up each like a jelly roll, starting with the long edge. Cut rolls into 1-inch slices. Place pieces sealed side down in pan or Dutch ovens. Cover and let rise until doubled in size, about ½ hour.

Bake in Dutch ovens for about 20 minutes, or in 375°F conventional oven for 25 minutes, or until golden brown.

Yield: 30 cinnamon rolls

SALADS

NOTE

During our twenty years of cooking outdoors, we've gathered some great salad and dressing recipes. While most of these don't require a Dutch oven for cooking, they make great accompaniments for Dutch oven meals. Some of the dressings are best made in a food processor, so you'll want to plan ahead before setting out on a camping or river trip. Here's a great way to store and transport pre-mixed dressings: Keep dressing in a tightly covered jar in refrigerator or cooler; shake vigorously before serving or tossing with salad ingredients.

POLLY'S CHINESE CHICKEN SALAD

Dressing:

6 large garlic cloves, peeled
2 tablespoons chopped, peeled fresh
    ginger root
1½ cups chopped fresh cilantro
1 tablespoon canola oil
1 tablespoon Oriental sesame oil
1 tablespoon hot chili oil
½ cup smooth, unsweetened peanut
    butter (natural variety)
½ cup soy sauce
1½ tablespoons sugar
3 tablespoons rice vinegar

Salad:

1½ pounds angel hair pasta
3 tablespoons Oriental sesame oil
¾ cup chopped fresh cilantro
1½ cups chopped scallions
3 stalks celery, chopped
4 cups chopped, cooked chicken
2 cups cashews, roasted and unsalted

Make the dressing: In a food processor, mince the garlic with ginger root and cilantro, then add canola oil, sesame oil and chili oil, peanut butter, soy sauce, sugar, and vinegar. Blend well. (If you're on the trail or don't have a food processor, you can mince garlic, ginger root, and cilantro together and whisk in other ingredients.) Covered and chilled, the sauce will keep for 1 month.

Make the salad: Cook pasta according to manufacturer's directions and drain. Rinse under cold water until it is cold. Toss pasta with oil, cilantro, scallions, celery, and chicken. The pasta may be prepared up to this point one day in advance if kept covered and chilled.

Just before serving, toss the pasta with the peanut sauce to coat it well, and garnish with cashews.

Yield: 15 servings

SALMON-STUFFED TOMATOES

1 can (16 ounces) pink salmon
3 scallions, chopped
2 stalks celery, chopped
½ cup chopped green olives
2 tablespoons Dijon mustard
¼ cup mayonnaise
1 teaspoon salt-free all purpose spice mix
6 large, ripe tomatoes
6 lettuce leaves
paprika for garnish

Combine salmon, scallions, celery, olives, mustard, mayonnaise, and spice mix. Mix well and set aside.

Section tomatoes into eighths without cutting all the way through. Spread each tomato open like a flower, and fill with one-sixth of the filling. Place on lettuce leaves and garnish with paprika.

Yield: 6 servings

CURRIED CHICKEN SALAD

This lowfat salad is a meal in itself and makes a perfect dinner for a warm evening.

4 boneless chicken breasts, skinned
4 tablespoons fresh chopped parsley
1 cup long-grain brown rice
2 cups unsalted chicken broth
2 medium onions, finely chopped
1 tablespoon canola oil
2 stalks celery, finely chopped
3 garlic cloves, finely minced
1 medium tomato, seeded and chopped
1 medium Granny Smith apple
1 tablespoon curry powder
¾ to 1 cup nonfat yogurt
freshly ground pepper to taste
parsley for garnish

Poach chicken, cool, and cut into bite-sized pieces. Combine with parsley and set aside. Cook rice in chicken broth.

Sauté onions in oil until tender. Add celery and cook 5 minutes longer. Mix in garlic and tomato. Cook 5 more minutes and remove from heat.

Core apple and cut into ¼-inch cubes. Add to vegetable mixture. Blend in curry powder and mix well. Add rice and vegetable mixture to chicken. Add yogurt and mix just until blended.

Adjust seasonings to taste. Sprinkle ground pepper and parsley on top. Serve at room temperature or chill before serving.

Yield: 6 servings

SHRIMP AND CABBAGE SALAD

Dressing:

1 envelope Hidden Valley Ranch dressing
1 cup whole milk
1 cup mayonnaise
1 avocado, peeled and mashed

Salad:

½ head green cabbage, chopped
½ head red cabbage, chopped
2 cans (6 ounces each) medium or large
    shrimp, drained

Make the dressing: Mix Hidden Valley Ranch dressing with milk and mayonnaise according to package directions. Combine with mashed avocado and set aside.

Make the salad: Combine green cabbage, red cabbage, and shrimp. Pour dressing over salad and toss.

Yield: 6 to 8 servings

TORTELLINI SALAD

1 cup chopped walnuts
2 packages (9 ounces each) fresh meat-
    or cheese-filled tortellini pasta,
    cooked and chilled
½ cup chopped scallions
½ red bell pepper, chopped
1 large tomato, chopped
2 stalks celery, chopped
pepper to taste
salt-free spice to taste
1 cup Dijon-type vinaigrette

Toast walnuts for 10 minutes in Dutch oven or for 10 minutes in 350°F conventional oven. Combine with rest of ingredients and toss. Chill before serving.

Yield: 6 servings

BLACK BEAN SALAD

2 cups dried black beans
3½ cups water
I cup chopped scallions
3 garlic cloves, crushed
I large carrot, chopped
2 tomatoes, chopped
I cup chopped cilantro
1½ teaspoons cumin
I teaspoon cayenne
I jar (12–16 ounces) salsa
lettuce for salad beds
yogurt and chips for garnish

Rinse black beans, put in a Dutch oven or large saucepan, and cover with water. Soak them several hours or overnight.

Pour off excess water, leaving enough to cover beans, and simmer beans 1½ hours over low heat. Drain and chill.

Toss beans with remaining ingredients. Serve on a bed of fresh lettuce with a dollop of yogurt on top and black bean tortilla chips on the side. This salad is also delicious stuffed into red bell peppers or tomatoes.

Yield: 6 servings

JALAPEÑO POTATO SALAD

Dressing:

4 tablespoons Dijon mustard
¼ cup wine vinegar
½ cup olive oil
2 garlic cloves, minced
salt and pepper to taste

Salad:

4 medium russet potatoes (unpeeled),
    cooked and cubed
I can medium, pitted black olives,
    chopped
6 jalapeño peppers, seeded and sliced
I cup chopped scallions
6 ounces feta cheese, crumbled

Mix dressing ingredients in a small bowl.

In a large bowl, combine potatoes, olives, peppers, scallions, and cheese. Pour dressing over all and toss. Adjust seasoning to taste.

Yield: 6 servings

POVERTY FLAT POTATO SALAD

Around 1900, Joe Groff worked a mining claim near the Main Salmon River. It had an open area known as Poverty Flat, where nothing would grow. This simple salad is named for the area.

4 medium-sized potatoes (unpeeled),
    cooked and cubed
1 red onion, chopped
3 stalks celery, chopped
½ cup chopped dill pickles
½ cup chopped green pepper
3 eggs, hard-cooked and cubed
½ cup mayonnaise
3 tablespoons Dijon mustard
1 teaspoon fresh ground pepper

Combine all ingredients and chill.

Yield: 6 to 8 servings

BLEU CHEESE WALNUT SALAD

1 cup broken walnut pieces
1 bunch leaf lettuce
1 Granny Smith apple, chopped
4 ounces bleu cheese, crumbled
1 cup Dijon-type vinaigrette

Toast walnuts for 10 minutes in Dutch oven or for 10 minutes in 350°F conventional oven. Tear the lettuce into pieces and toss with nuts and remaining ingredients.

Yield: 6 servings

WILD RICE SALAD

Salad:

1 cup uncooked wild rice
2 cups chicken broth
1 cup snow peas, cut in bite-sized pieces
6 scallions, chopped
½ cup chopped red bell pepper
¼ cup sliced water chestnuts
½ cup sliced mushrooms
1 can black olives, sliced in half

Dressing:

⅓ cup tarragon vinegar
1 teaspoon salt (optional)
1 teaspoon dried tarragon leaves
¼ cup safflower oil or olive oil

My sister-in-law, Betty Mills, uses wild rice grown by her friends in St. Maries, Idaho, to complement the nutty flavor of this salad.

Boil rice in chicken broth for 10 minutes and reduce to simmer for 40 minutes or until rice is rather nutty in texture. Drain and cool. (Rice can be cooked ahead of time and stored in a cooler or refrigerator.)

Add peas, scallions, bell pepper, water chestnuts, mushrooms, and black olives. Stir and set aside.

In a small bowl, combine dressing ingredients. Pour over salad and toss. Chill before serving.

Yield: 6 servings

BROCCOLI WITH DIJON VINAIGRETTE

2 pounds fresh broccoli florets
4 teaspoons olive oil
¼ cup finely chopped scallions
½ teaspoon dried tarragon
½ teaspoon dry mustard
3 garlic cloves, minced
2 tablespoons balsamic vinegar
2 tablespoons water
1 tablespoon Dijon mustard
¼ teaspoon ground pepper
⅛ teaspoon salt

Steam broccoli for 6 minutes or until crisp-tender. Drain and put into a bowl. Heat olive oil in skillet and sauté scallions, tarragon, dry mustard, and garlic for 3 minutes.

Remove from heat and add vinegar, water, Dijon mustard, pepper, and salt, stirring until blended. Drizzle over broccoli, tossing to coat. Serve while warm.

Yield: 8 servings

HEARTS OF PALM AND PEPPER SALAD

1 bunch leaf lettuce
1 can (12–14 ounces) hearts of palm,
    sliced into ½-inch pieces
1 red bell pepper, seeded and sliced in strips
1 jar capers, drained
½ cup Dijon-type vinaigrette
freshly ground black pepper to taste

Tear the lettuce into pieces and toss with palm, peppers, capers, and vinaigrette. Top with pepper to taste.

Yield: 6 servings

BIG CREEK BROCCOLI SALAD

My good friend Catherine Scott, a home designer in Boise, shared this great recipe with me. Big Creek is a major tributary in Impassable Canyon on the Middle Fork of the Salmon River.

Combine vegetables and sunflower seeds. In a separate bowl, combine dressing ingredients. Pour over vegetables and toss. Chill before serving.

Yield: 6 to 8 servings

Salad:

½ head cauliflower, cut into
    small florets
½ head broccoli, cut into small florets
2 medium-sized tomatoes, cut into chunks
1 small red onion, chopped
1 can black olives, drained and chopped
½ cup sunflower seeds
1 cup peas (frozen or fresh), blanched and
    chilled

Dressing:

¼ cup wine vinegar
¼ cup olive oil
⅛ teaspoon mustard seed
⅛ teaspoon celery seed
1 teaspoon sweet basil
salt and pepper to taste

ORANGE PECAN SALAD

This is great served with Sheila's Honey Mustard Dressing (recipe on page 62).

1 cup pecan pieces
1 can (8 ounces) mandarin oranges, or 2
    fresh oranges, peeled and sectioned
1 bunch leaf lettuce
½ red onion, thinly sliced
1 bunch radishes, thinly sliced

Toast pecans for 10 minutes in Dutch oven or for 10 minutes in a 350°F conventional oven. Toss with remaining ingredients. Chill before serving.

Yield: 6 servings

SHEILA'S HONEY MUSTARD DRESSING

3 tablespoons, plus 1 teaspoon Dijon
    mustard
7 tablespoons honey
½ cup apple cider vinegar
1 cup oil (canola or olive)

Mix all ingredients very well.

Yield: Slightly less than 1 cup

SPICY BUTTERMILK DRESSING

I cup buttermilk
I tablespoon Dijon-style mustard
I tablespoon minced onion
¼ teaspoon dried dill weed
I tablespoon chopped fresh parsley
⅛ teaspoon salt
⅛ teaspoon black pepper

Combine all ingredients in a jar, cover, and shake to blend. Adjust spices to taste. Chill. Shake well again before using.

Yield: 1 cup

GREEN'S SALAD DRESSING FOR GREENS

My friend Melissa Green prepares this great dressing in advance for river trips.

I egg
2 ounces Parmesan cheese, grated
    (½ cup)
¼ cup lemon juice
2 garlic cloves, minced
I teaspoon Worcestershire sauce
½ teaspoon pepper
½ cup olive oil

Blend egg, Parmesan, lemon juice, garlic, Worcestershire, and pepper at low speed. Add olive oil and blend again. Chill 1 hour before serving.

Yield: about 1 cup

APPETIZERS, SNACKS, AND SANDWICHES

REMEMBER

When a recipe calls for baking, braising, stewing, or roasting, the Dutch oven must be covered with charcoal briquettes on top of the lid. For boiling, frying, sautéing, and quick-heating, leave the Dutch oven cover off. For more on cooking techniques for the Dutch oven, see "Dutch Oven Care and Use," pages 2–3.

BASIL PESTO DIP

Pesto:

5 garlic cloves
¾ cup firmly packed fresh basil leaves
3 tablespoons almonds, blanched
3 tablespoons olive oil
3 ounces Parmesan cheese, grated
    (¾ cup)

24 ounces whole milk ricotta cheese, at
    room temperature

Make the pesto: Place the garlic, basil, and almonds in the bowl of a food processor or blender. With the motor running, slowly drizzle in the oil through the feed tube. Process until the basil is pureed. Transfer the pesto to a bowl and stir in the Parmesan cheese. (The pesto can be refrigerated for up to three days.)

To complete the dip, beat ricotta and pesto in a mixer or food processor until well blended. Cover and chill until ready to use. Serve on crackers, toasted French bread, or stuffed into cherry tomatoes.

Yield: 4 cups

CHILI CHEESE DIP

2 pounds Velveeta cheese, cubed
4 cans (14–16 ounces each) chili
    without beans
2 cans (7 ounces each) chopped
    green chiles

Mix all ingredients, then heat slowly in Dutch oven, saucepan, or microwave until melted. Stir again. Serve warm with tortilla chips.

Yield: about 8 cups

PAPAYA SALSA

This salsa is great served with grilled fish or pork, or any dish you want to give a tropical flavor.

3 medium-sized cucumbers, peeled and diced
3 fresh jalapeño peppers, seeded and minced
1 medium-sized yellow or white onion, minced
3 papayas, peeled and cubed
2 mangos, peeled and cubed (as best you can)
2 cans (20 ounces each) crushed or diced pineapple, drained
½ cup fresh lime juice
1 red bell pepper, chopped
3 kiwis, peeled and chopped

Combine all ingredients, cover, and chill.

Yield: 7 to 8 cups

OLIVADA

1 cup pimiento-stuffed green olives
1 cup Kalamata olives, pitted
1 cup black olives, pitted
1 tablespoon capers
1 tablespoon olive oil
½ cup tomatillo salsa

Blend all ingredients in food processor. Refrigerate. Serve on French bread or crackers, or use as a sandwich spread.

Yield: 3 cups

GREEN SALSA

Karen Vorster, a river guide and ski patroller, gave me this great salsa recipe. Prepare this ahead of time at home before you go camping or on a river trip.

2 fresh jalapeño peppers, seeded
4 to 6 fresh Anaheim peppers, seeded
6 green peppers, seeded
4 garlic cloves, peeled
2 avocados, peeled and pitted
2 tablespoons chopped cilantro
1 tablespoon olive oil
dash fresh lime juice

Blend all ingredients in a blender until smooth. Serve with tortilla tips.

Yield: about 2 cups

NOT-FOR-THE-FAINTHEARTED NACHOS

2 large heads of garlic, peeled and separated into cloves
2 tablespoons olive oil
1 package (10 ounces) tortilla chips
¼ cup chopped red onion
1 can (4 ounces) green chiles, chopped
⅓ cup pimiento-stuffed green olives, sliced
6 ounces Monterey Jack cheese, grated (1½ cups)
chopped cilantro and chopped scallions for garnish

Coat garlic cloves with olive oil, cover, and bake in Dutch oven for 30 minutes, or in 350°F conventional oven for 30 minutes, or until soft and golden.

Cover the bottom of 12" Dutch oven or 9"x 12" baking pan with tortilla chips.

Mash the garlic, and mix in onion, chiles, and olives. Spread evenly over chips and cover with cheese. Bake in Dutch oven or in 375°F conventional oven for 5 minutes, or until cheese melts. Top with cilantro and scallions.

Yield: 6 servings

CRAB-STUFFED MUSHROOMS

12 large mushrooms
2 tablespoons minced scallions (use green part)
2 tablespoons plus 3 tablespoons butter
1 teaspoon lemon juice
1 cup flaked, cooked crab meat
½ cup wheat germ
½ cup sour cream
3 ounces Swiss cheese, grated (¾ cup)
¼ cup dry white wine
lemon wedges for garnish

Wipe mushrooms with a damp cloth. Remove and finely chop the stems. Sauté mushroom stems and scallions in 2 tablespoons of the butter until onion is limp. Remove from heat and stir in lemon juice, crab meat, wheat germ, sour cream, and a third of the cheese.

Melt remaining 3 tablespoons butter in Dutch oven or 9" x 12" baking dish. Turn mushroom caps in the butter until well coated. Spoon about 2 tablespoons of the crab meat mixture into each cap. Place mushrooms, filled side up, in Dutch oven or dish.

Before baking, sprinkle mushrooms with the remaining cheese and pour wine around mushrooms in bottom of Dutch oven or dish.

Bake in Dutch oven for 10 to 15 minutes, or in 350°F conventional oven for 15 to 20 minutes. Serve hot with lemon wedges.

Yield: 6 servings

MUSHROOMS AU GRATIN

1 pound fresh mushrooms
2 tablespoons butter
⅓ cup sour cream
¼ teaspoon salt
dash pepper
1 tablespoon unbleached all-purpose flour
¼ cup chopped parsley
2 ounces Swiss or mild Cheddar cheese,
     grated (½ cup)

Slice mushrooms lengthwise in ¼-inch pieces. Heat butter in skillet or Dutch oven over medium heat; sauté mushrooms. Cover pan for about 2 minutes until the mushrooms begin to exude juices.

In a separate bowl, blend sour cream, salt, pepper, and flour until smooth. Stir into mushroom mixture in pan and heat, stirring, until blended and beginning to boil.

Sprinkle parsley and cheese over mixture and heat until cheese melts, about 10 minutes. Serve with crackers or toasted French bread.

Yield: 4 servings

CHEDDAR BISCUITS WITH HAM

These biscuits make a delicious appetizer. Serve them hot out of the oven.

1¾ cups unbleached all-purpose flour
2 teaspoons baking powder
1 teaspoon salt
3 tablespoons unsalted butter
2 ounces Cheddar cheese, grated (½ cup)
¾ cup buttermilk
½ cup chopped green scallions
8 tablespoons (1 stick) butter
½ pound Black Forest ham or any good-
    quality ham, thinly sliced

Line a baking sheet or two Dutch ovens with parchment paper.

In a large bowl, combine flour, baking powder, and salt. Add butter and blend with a pastry blender or your fingers until mixture resembles coarse meal. Stir in cheese. Add buttermilk and scallions and mix well.

Roll out dough to ½-inch thickness. Cut out biscuits using 1½-inch round cutter. Gather scraps, reroll, and cut again, using all of the dough. Place biscuits on parchment paper (they should not touch each other).

Bake in Dutch oven or in 350°F conventional oven for about 15 minutes, or until biscuits are puffed and light golden. Cool.

Split and lightly butter biscuits. Stuff with ham slices. Return biscuits to Dutch ovens or conventional oven and bake 5 minutes or until heated through.

Yield: about 35 biscuits

BRUSCHETTA WITH SUMMER TOMATOES

This traditional grilled Italian treat tastes great made with vine-ripe tomatoes.

2 garlic cloves, finely chopped
3 ripe red tomatoes, coarsely chopped
    and drained
¼ cup chopped fresh basil
¼ cup chopped fresh parsley
⅓ cup olive oil
½ teaspoon salt
½ teaspoon freshly ground black pepper
8 thick slices crusty Italian or French
    bread

Combine all ingredients except bread and set aside.

Grill bread slices on both sides until crispy. Top with tomato mixture and serve immediately.

Yield: 8 servings

CRACKER BREAD SANDWICHES

Serve this as an appetizer or for lunch.

3 rounds Middle Eastern cracker bread
    (14-inch diameter)
10 ounces cream cheese, softened
1 package (6 ounces) alfalfa sprouts
4 ripe tomatoes, thinly sliced
4 avocados, peeled, pitted, and thinly
    sliced
2 medium-sized cucumbers, thinly sliced
12 ounces Cheddar cheese, grated
    (3 cups)
1 can (12–14 ounces) black olives,
    chopped

Follow package directions for preparing cracker bread.

Spread one layer of cracker bread with cream cheese, then layer the sprouts and tomatoes. Place another cracker on top and layer with avocados, cucumbers, cheddar cheese, and olives. Top with third cracker and cut into squares or wedges.

Yield: 10 to 12 servings

ASPARAGUS AND CHEESE SANDWICHES

4 whole wheat English muffins, halved
1 package (10 ounces) frozen asparagus
　　spears, thawed and drained
1 can (12–14 ounces) pitted black olives,
　　sliced
16 ounces Swiss cheese, sliced or grated
　　(4 cups)
1 envelope premixed, dry Hollandaise
　　sauce, or Jiffy Hollandaise (recipe
　　below)
paprika for garnish

Toast muffins in Dutch oven or under broiler. Arrange asparagus, olives, and cheese on muffins. Bake from top and bottom in Dutch oven or put under broiler in conventional oven until cheese melts.

Prepare Hollandaise sauce, drizzle sauce over each muffin half, and sprinkle with paprika.

Yield: 6 to 8 servings

JIFFY HOLLANDAISE

¼ cup sour cream
¼ cup mayonnaise
½ teaspoon mustard
1 teaspoon lemon juice

Combine all ingredients. Cook and stir over low heat until heated through.

Yield: ½ cup

GRILLED CHEESE AND AVOCADO SANDWICHES

8 slices whole wheat bread
4 tablespoons butter
4 large slices Cheddar cheese
2 ripe avocados, sliced
3 ounces cream cheese, softened

Butter both sides of bread. Layer cheese, avocados, and cream cheese on one slice bread and top with another slice.

Grill in skillet, on Dutch oven lid, or in bottom of Dutch oven until bread is golden brown and cheese is melted. Cut sandwiches in half and serve.

Yield: 4 servings

GRILLED CREAM CHEESE AND OLIVE SANDWICHES

8 slices whole wheat bread
4 tablespoons butter
8 ounces cream cheese, softened
1 can (10–12 ounces) pitted black olives, sliced

Butter both sides of bread. Spread cream cheese generously on four slices bread. Sprinkle olive slices over cream cheese. Top with another slice of bread.

Grill in skillet, on Dutch oven lid, or in bottom of Dutch oven until bread is golden brown and cheese is soft. Cut sandwiches in half and serve.

Yield: 4 servings

POULTRY AND
FISH DISHES

REMEMBER

When a recipe calls for baking, braising, stewing, or roasting, the Dutch oven must be covered with charcoal briquettes on top of the lid. For boiling, frying, sautéing, and quick-heating, leave the Dutch oven cover off. For more on cooking techniques for the Dutch oven, see "Dutch Oven Care and Use," pages 2–3.

CHICKEN CACCIATORE

This is a family recipe from Cornellia Caccia, a Pocatello chef responsible for the success of several Italian restaurants in southeastern Idaho. Cornellia's nephew, John Caccia, likes to prepare and freeze this dish in advance. He also suggests expanding your horizons by substituting venison, pheasant, duck, or rabbit for the classic chicken.

6 garlic cloves, sliced

1 large onion, sliced

1½ teaspoons dried oregano leaves

1½ teaspoons chopped fresh sweet basil

1 teaspoon chopped fresh parsley

1 teaspoon anise seeds

1 cup mushrooms, cut in half

3 tablespoons plus 1 tablespoon olive oil

1 large cut-up chicken (or equivalent quantity of venison, pheasant, duck, rabbit)

3 cans (6 ounces each) tomato paste

5 cans (8 ounces each) tomato sauce

1 cup water

1 can (6 ounces) pitted black olives, drained

2 tablespoons sugar

½ teaspoon salt

½ teaspoon pepper

2 tablespoons grated Parmesan cheese

5 whole bay leaves

In a large Dutch oven, sauté garlic, onion, oregano leaves, basil, parsley, anise seeds, and mushrooms in 3 tablespoons of the olive oil. Set aside.

In a frying pan, brown chicken in remaining tablespoon of oil. In a separate bowl, mix tomato paste, tomato sauce, water, olives, sugar, salt, pepper, Parmesan, and bay leaves. Add the browned chicken and tomato sauce mixture to the Dutch oven. Simmer for 3 hours. Remove bay leaves.

When properly cooked, the chicken meat will just fall off the bones. Serve over noodles or cornbread. You can use any leftover sauce to make pizza.

Variation: A great vegetarian adaptation to this hunter-style Italian dish was given to me by John's brother, Bill Caccia, a longtime friend. Refer to page 126 for Tofu Cacciatore recipe.

Yield: 6 servings

SAUCY CHICKEN

This dish is wonderful served warm with corn bread on the side. For a unique sandwich, pile the chicken mixture between two slices of corn bread.

6 chicken breasts, skinned, trimmed of excess fat, split, and halved
2 tablespoons olive oil
I large onion, chopped
2 medium shallots, minced
2 tablespoons unsalted butter
12 ounces mushrooms, sliced
2 tablespoons unbleached all-purpose flour
⅓ cup dry white wine
2 cups chicken stock or canned low-sodium broth
½ cup low-fat sour cream
salt and pepper to taste
2 jars (4 ounces each) pimientos, drained and diced
2 tablespoons minced cilantro

Brown chicken in oil until partially cooked. Set aside. Cook onion and shallots in butter until softened and slightly browned. Add mushrooms and cook for 6 to 8 minutes. Stir in flour and cook for an additional 5 minutes. Add wine and cook until the mixture becomes thick and pasty.

Gradually add the chicken stock or broth, stirring until stock is thickened slightly. Stir in sour cream and adjust seasoning with salt and pepper to taste. Stir in pimientos and cilantro.

Cut the chicken off the bones, add to sauce, and let cook about 5 minutes or until chicken is cooked through.

Yield: 6 to 8 servings

AIOLI CENTENNIAL CHICKEN

This garlic lover's delight was created to help celebrate Idaho's Centennial in July of 1990. The aioli works best when made in a food processor; prepare it ahead and keep cold until ready to use.

1 slice French bread, crust discarded
5 to 6 garlic cloves, crushed
2 egg yolks
1 teaspoon fresh lemon juice
pinch salt
pinch white pepper
¾ cup olive oil
4 whole, boneless, skinless chicken breasts
    (about 2½ pounds)
¼ teaspoon black pepper

To make aioli, soak bread in water and squeeze it dry. Place in food processor. Add garlic, egg yolks, lemon juice, salt, and white pepper. Purée mixture until smooth. With processor motor on, add olive oil slowly in a thin stream. Purée until mixture has the consistency of mayonnaise.

Cut chicken breasts in half. Lightly pound each until ½ inch thick. Spread aioli on both sides and sprinkle with pepper.

For Dutch oven cooking, place chicken in Dutch oven with maximum heat on top and broil until pieces are slightly browned and cooked thoroughly. For conventional cooking, place chicken in 2-quart casserole dish, bake uncovered at 400°F for 20 minutes, cover and reduce heat to 350°F, and bake for 10 more minutes.

Yield: 6 servings

CHICKEN CURRY

¼ cup olive oil
¼ cup red curry paste (available at Asian markets)
2 teaspoons curry powder
6 tablespoons fermented fish sauce (available at Asian markets)
1 chicken breast, boned and sliced
2 potatoes, peeled and cut into 16 to 20 slices
2 carrots, cut into 16 to 20 slices
4 cups coconut milk

Heat the oil and add curry paste and curry powder. Stir-fry over high heat for 1 minute. Add the fish sauce, chicken, potatoes, and carrots. Stir-fry until chicken is reddish brown. Add the coconut milk and bring to a boil. Reduce heat, cover, and simmer for 30 minutes.

Yield: 4 servings

GRILLED YOGURT-ENCRUSTED CORNISH HENS WITH COUSCOUS

2 cups plain, nonfat yogurt
2 tablespoons minced garlic
2 tablespoons chopped ginger root
2 tablespoons olive oil
¼ cup curry powder, or to taste
4 Cornish hens, split in half, with skin removed
1 package (10½ ounces) couscous, cooked according to package directions
yogurt, fresh cilantro, chutney, peanuts, and/or sesame seeds for garnish

The yogurt marinade tenderizes the hens and forms a great crust during grilling. Chicken pieces may be used in lieu of Cornish hens.

In a food processor or with a whisk, combine yogurt, garlic, ginger root, and olive oil until smooth. Blend in curry powder. Pour over hens and marinate, covered, in refrigerator or cooler for 12 hours. Occasionally stir or shake container to coat thoroughly.

Remove from refrigerator or cooler about 30 minutes before cooking. Grill over hot coals until browned and done, about 10 minutes on each side. Serve hot or at room temperature with prepared couscous and condiments such as plain yogurt, chopped cilantro, chutney, chopped peanuts, or toasted sesame seeds.

Yield: 4 to 8 servings

SARA'S CHICKEN

This unique Dutch oven dish is named after Sara Biddle, a special guest of Middle Fork Wilderness Outfitters. It's great served with fresh spinach fettucini, Caesar salad, and steamed carrots.

8 chicken breasts, boned and skinned
1 cup plus ½ cup unbleached all-purpose
    flour
1 teaspoon freshly ground pepper
oil for greasing pan
½ cup olive oil
½ cup butter
½ pound pancetta, diced
8 shallots, sliced
1 ½ pounds fresh mushrooms, sliced
1 cup tarragon vinegar
1 cup sweet vermouth
½ teaspoon dried tarragon
16 ounces mozzarella cheese, sliced
2 tomatoes, diced
¼ cup chopped fresh parsley

Dredge chicken breasts in 1 cup of the flour and pepper, then brown them in a skillet in oil and butter. Place breasts in a lightly oiled Dutch oven.

In a separate pan, heat olive oil and sauté pancetta, shallots, and mushrooms until soft. Add ½ cup flour to mixture so it is sticky, not dry. Pour vinegar over mixture (most will evaporate). Pour vermouth on top. At this point the mixture should be moist but not watery. Add tarragon.

Spoon mushroom mixture over chicken and place a slice of mozzarella over each breast.

Bake in Dutch oven for 35 minutes, or cover and bake in 350°F conventional oven for 30 to 40 minutes.

Top with tomatoes and parsley. Cover and cook for another 10 minutes.

Yield: 8 servings

BAKED WHEAT GERM CHICKEN

1 large, three-drumstick frying chicken
½ cup butter, melted
1 cup wheat germ
salt and pepper to taste
paprika to taste

Skin and dry the chicken pieces. Roll each in the melted butter and then dip into the wheat germ to coat. Place pieces in the bottom of a Dutch oven or in a baking dish. Pour remaining butter over chicken and season with salt and pepper. Garnish with paprika.

Bake for 40 to 45 minutes in the Dutch oven, or for 45 to 50 minutes in a 350°F conventional oven.

Yield: 4 to 6 servings

CRAB-STUFFED CHICKEN BREASTS

4 large whole chicken breasts, halved,
    skinned, and boned
3 tablespoons plus 1 tablespoon butter or
    margarine
¼ cup unbleached all-purpose flour
¾ cup milk
¾ cup chicken broth
⅓ cup dry white wine
¼ cup chopped scallions
1 can (7½ ounces) crab meat
4 ounces fresh mushrooms, chopped
½ cup wheat germ
2 tablespoons snipped fresh parsley
½ teaspoon salt
dash pepper
4 ounces Swiss cheese, grated (1 cup)
½ teaspoon paprika

Place each chicken piece, boned side up, between two pieces of waxed paper. Working from the center out, pound each piece lightly with a meat mallet to make cutlet about ⅛ inch thick. Set aside.

In a saucepan, melt 3 tablespoons of the butter or margarine. Blend in flour.

In a separate bowl, stir together milk, chicken broth, and wine. Pour into butter-flour mixture in saucepan. Cook and stir until sauce thickens and bubbles. Set aside.

Sauté scallions in the remaining 1 tablespoon of butter until tender but not brown. Stir in crab meat, mushrooms, wheat germ, parsley, salt, and pepper. Stir in 2 tablespoons of the sauce. Top each chicken piece with about ¼ cup of the crab meat mixture. Fold sides in and roll up. Place rolls seam side down in a Dutch oven. Pour remaining sauce over all.

Bake, covered, in 350°F conventional oven for 1 hour or until chicken is tender, or in Dutch oven with coals on top and bottom for 40 to 45 minutes. Uncover and sprinkle with cheese and paprika. Bake 2 minutes longer or until cheese melts.

Yield: 8 servings

COQ AU VIN

6 uncooked bacon slices, diced
²⁄₃ cup sliced scallions
1 (about 2½ pounds) fryer chicken, cut up
   (or 3 breasts, halved, or 3 drumsticks
   and 3 thighs)
8 small white onions, peeled
8 ounces whole mushrooms
1 garlic clove, crushed
1 teaspoon salt
¼ teaspoon pepper
½ teaspoon dried thyme
8 small potatoes, scrubbed
2 cups Burgundy wine
1 cup chicken broth
chopped parsley for garnish

In a Dutch oven or large skillet, sauté diced bacon and scallions until bacon is crisp. Remove and drain on a paper towel, leaving 2 tablespoons of bacon grease in skillet.

Put chicken pieces in skillet and brown well on all sides. Remove the chicken and set aside.

Put peeled whole onions, mushrooms, and garlic in Dutch oven or 2-quart casserole dish. Add the browned chicken pieces, bacon and scallions, salt, pepper, thyme, potatoes, wine, and chicken broth.

Bake for 1 hour in Dutch oven on medium heat, or cover and bake for 1 hour in 350°F conventional oven. Garnish with chopped parsley.

Yield: 6 servings

MUSHROOM-STUFFED CHICKEN BREASTS WITH ARTICHOKES

8 ounces fresh mushrooms, sliced
2 tablespoons plus 4 tablespoons mar-
    garine
6 to 8 chicken breasts, boned and skinned
½ teaspoon paprika
¼ teaspoon pepper
1 package frozen artichoke hearts, thawed
    and drained
2 tablespoons unbleached all-purpose
    flour
⅔ cup chicken broth
⅔ cup dry sherry
salt to taste

Sauté mushrooms in 2 tablespoons of the margarine until browned. Place each chicken breast, boned side down, between two pieces of waxed paper. Pound each breast lightly with a meat mallet. Put mushrooms in the center of each breast, using all mushrooms, and roll up.

Heat 4 tablespoons margarine in a large skillet or Dutch oven, place breasts fold side down in pan, and brown. Sprinkle breasts with paprika and pepper. Arrange breasts and artichokes in a Dutch oven or a large, shallow baking dish.

Stir flour into margarine remaining in pan and gradually add broth and sherry. Bring to boil, stirring constantly. Add salt to taste. Pour sauce over chicken and artichokes.

Bake 45 minutes in Dutch oven, or for 1 hour in a 375°F conventional oven, basting occasionally.

Yield: 6 servings

POLLY BEMIS CHICKEN

As a young Chinese woman, Polly Bemis was sold as a slave and later was won in a poker game by Charles Bemis, who eventually married her. Charles and Polly moved to the banks of the Salmon River in 1894, and Polly continued to live there until 1923. She was a hard worker, growing a productive garden, cutting firewood, cooking, and caring for livestock. Polly Creek on the Main Salmon River is named for her.

1 (3 pound) fryer chicken, cut in eight pieces
2 tablespoons olive oil
1 teaspoon salt
1 jar (8 ounces) orange marmalade
1 bottle (8 ounces) Russian dressing
1 fresh orange, peeled and thinly sliced

Brown chicken in oil in bottom of Dutch oven. Sprinkle with salt. Pour the marmalade and Russian dressing over chicken and arrange the orange slices on top.

Bake in Dutch oven for 40 to 45 minutes, or in 375°F conventional oven for 50 to 60 minutes.

Yield: 4 to 6 servings

STICKY CHICKEN

My aunt, Mac Oliver, found this recipe in her local newspaper. She often substitutes pheasant for the chicken, with delicious results.

1 jar (8 ounces) apricot or pineapple jam
½ envelope dry Lipton onion soup mix
1 bottle (8 ounces) spicy French dressing
1 large chicken, cut into eight pieces
salt and pepper to taste

Mix together the jam, dry soup, and French dressing. Chill for one hour or longer to blend the flavors.

Place chicken parts in a Dutch oven or 2-quart casserole dish and pour sauce over them. Season with salt and pepper to taste.

Bake in Dutch oven for 45 to 50 minutes, or cover and bake in 350°F conventional oven for 50 to 60 minutes, or until tender.

Yield: 6 servings

THUNDER MOUNTAIN CHICKEN AND BROCCOLI

In 1900, Thunder Mountain was a booming gold mining area on Monumental Creek in the Salmon River Wilderness.

2 cups Medium White Sauce (recipe
   follows)
2 tablespoons Beau Monde seasoning
$\frac{1}{2}$ teaspoon salt
3 pounds chicken meat, boned and cubed
1 bunch broccoli, cut into 2-inch pieces
paprika to taste

Prepare white sauce and add seasoning mix and salt. Mix well. Arrange chicken and broccoli in Dutch oven or 2-quart casserole dish and pour sauce over the top. Sprinkle with paprika.

Bake in Dutch oven for 1 hour at moderate heat, or in 350°F conventional oven for 1 hour.

Yield: 6 to 8 servings

MEDIUM WHITE SAUCE

4 tablespoons butter or margarine
4 tablespoons unbleached all-purpose
   flour
$\frac{1}{2}$ teaspoon salt
dash pepper
2 cups milk

Melt butter in saucepan over low heat. Blend in flour, salt, and pepper. Add milk all at once. Cook at medium heat, stirring constantly, until mixture thickens and bubbles. Remove sauce from heat when it bubbles. If sauce cooks too long, it will become too thick and the butter will separate. (If this happens, you can repair it by stirring in a little more milk and cooking, stirring constantly, until sauce bubbles.)

Yield: 3 cups

CREAMY CHICKEN ENCHILADAS

½ pound skinless, boneless chicken
    breasts, steamed or baked
1 package (10 ounces) frozen chopped
    spinach, thawed and well drained
¼ cup thinly sliced scallions
1 cup sour cream
¼ cup plain yogurt
2 tablespoons unbleached all-purpose
    flour
¼ teaspoon ground cumin
salt to taste
¼ cup milk
1 can (4 ounces) diced green chili pep-
    pers, drained
6 flour tortillas, 7-inch diameter
3 ounces Monterey Jack cheese, grated
    (⅓ cup)
salsa and chopped scallions for garnish

Shred cooked chicken into bite-size pieces. Combine chicken, spinach, and scallions; set aside.

In a separate bowl combine sour cream, yogurt, flour, cumin, and salt. Stir in milk and chili peppers. Divide sauce in half.

Combine chicken mixture and half the sauce. Divide this filling among the tortillas and roll them up. Place rolled tortillas in the bottom of a Dutch oven or baking pan. Spoon the remaining sauce over the enchiladas.

Bake in Dutch oven for 25 to 30 minutes, or in 350°F conventional oven for 30 minutes. Sprinkle with the cheese and let stand for 5 minutes. To serve, garnish with salsa and additional chopped scallions.

Yield: 6 servings

CHICKEN AND ASPARAGUS STIR-FRY

I pound boneless, skinless chicken
    breasts, cut into 1-inch thick strips
I tablespoon plus 2 teaspoons cornstarch
I teaspoon plus 2 teaspoons vegetable oil
¼ teaspoon salt
⅛ teaspoon freshly ground black pepper
½ pound fresh asparagus
I cup chicken broth
I teaspoon sugar
I teaspoon sesame oil
I teaspoon soy sauce
½ red bell pepper, finely chopped
I piece (1 inch long) fresh ginger root,
    peeled and finely chopped
2 garlic cloves, finely chopped
¼ teaspoon cayenne pepper

Combine chicken, 1 tablespoon of the cornstarch, 1 teaspoon of the vegetable oil, salt, and black pepper. Cover and chill for 15 minutes.

In a large skillet or Dutch oven, heat ¼ inch of water to boiling. Break off woody ends of asparagus and cut each spear crosswise into 1-inch pieces. Add asparagus pieces to water and cook 2 to 3 minutes or until almost tender. Drain and set aside.

In a small bowl, combine broth, the remaining cornstarch, sugar, sesame oil, and soy sauce; set aside.

Heat the remaining 2 teaspoons vegetable oil and add red bell pepper and ginger root. Stir-fry 1 minute. Add garlic and cayenne and stir-fry another 30 seconds. Add chicken and stir-fry 3 minutes.

Stir in broth mixture and heat until thickened and chicken is cooked through, about 2 minutes. Stir in asparagus and heat through. Serve immediately.

Yield: 4 servings

CHICKEN WITH DRIED FRUIT SAUCE

Chicken:

4 (4 ounces each) skinned, boned chicken
    breast halves
1/2 teaspoon salt
1/4 teaspoon pepper
2 teaspoons margarine

Dried Fruit Sauce:

1 cup mixed dried fruit bits
3/4 cup Riesling or other sweet white wine
1/4 cup water
5 whole cloves
2 cinnamon sticks
1 tablespoon brown sugar
1/2 teaspoon cornstarch

Place chicken breasts between sheets of waxed paper and pound to 1/4-inch thickness. Sprinkle breasts with salt and pepper.

Melt margarine in Dutch oven. Add chicken and cook 3 minutes on each side. Set chicken aside and keep warm.

Make the sauce: Add dried fruit bits, wine, water, cloves, and cinnamon sticks to Dutch oven and bring to boil. Add brown sugar and cornstach. Cook 1 minute, stirring constantly. Discard cloves and cinnamon sticks. Pour sauce over chicken before serving.

Yield: 4 servings

MELISSA'S CHICKEN

My longtime friend and river runner Melissa Green shared this easy, delicious Dutch oven chicken dish with me.

4 whole chicken breasts, halved, skinned
    and boned
2 eggs, beaten
bread crumbs for coating chicken
butter and olive oil, as needed
16 ounces marinara sauce
1/2 cup milk
8 thin slices Swiss cheese
8 thin slices mozzarella cheese
2 ounces Parmesan cheese, grated
    (1/2 cup)

Dip chicken breasts in egg and roll in bread crumbs to coat. Fry chicken in butter and olive oil.

In a small bowl, dilute marinara sauce with milk. Cover bottom of Dutch oven or 2-quart casserole dish with sauce mixture. Layer chicken on top of sauce. Top with slices of Swiss and mozzarella cheese. Sprinkle Parmesan over all.

Bake in Dutch oven for 30 minutes, or cover and bake in 350°F conventional oven for 30 minutes. Uncover partially and cook 10 more minutes.

Yield: 6 to 8 servings

CHICKEN WITH SHIITAKE MUSHROOMS

1 teaspoon vegetable oil
10 ounces shiitake mushrooms
2 medium shallots, minced
¼ garlic clove, minced
2 tablespoons dry white wine
2 tablespoons chopped fresh parsley
juice of ½ lemon
4 boneless chicken breasts, skin removed
2 tablespoons balsamic vinegar
10 ounces chicken stock or broth
2 tablespoons olive oil
1 tablespoon chopped fresh thyme
1 tablespoon chopped fresh tarragon
1 tablespoon chopped chives

Heat oil in a Dutch oven or oven-proof skillet until very hot. Sauté mushrooms, shallots, and garlic until wilted. Deglaze Dutch oven with white wine. Remove from heat and fold in parsley and lemon juice.

Cut a small pocket into the side of each chicken breast. Divide mushroom mixture into quarters and stuff into pockets. Tie with string to keep in place. Sauté breasts until golden on both sides.

Bake in Dutch oven for 10 to 12 minutes, or in 375°F conventional oven for 15 minutes. Remove chicken from Dutch oven or skillet; pour off excess fat.

Deglaze Dutch oven or skillet with vinegar and chicken stock or broth. Reduce drippings by half, then whip in olive oil, thyme, tarragon, and chives. Pour over chicken and serve.

Yield: 4 servings

BAKED CHICKEN AND NOODLES

You can make a low-fat version of this recipe by using nonfat dairy products and mayonnaise.

1 cup cottage cheese
½ cup cream cheese, softened
½ cup mayonnaise
½ cup chopped onion
½ cup chopped green bell pepper
¼ cup minced parsley
2 tablespoons margarine
⅓ cup unbleached all-purpose flour
½ cup milk
1 can (10½ ounces) low-salt chicken broth
½ teaspoon poultry seasoning
¼ teaspoon salt
¼ teaspoon pepper
dash garlic powder
8 to 10 cooked lasagna noodles
3 cups diced cooked chicken breast
½ cup dry bread crumbs
2 tablespoons chopped parsley
¼ teaspoon paprika

Combine cottage cheese, cream cheese, and mayonnaise, and beat well. Stir in onion, bell pepper, and ¼ cup parsley; set aside.

Melt margarine and add flour, cooking 1 minute, stirring constantly. Add milk and chicken broth. Bring to a boil and cook 3 minutes until thickened, stirring constantly. Stir in poultry seasoning, salt, pepper, and garlic powder. Set sauce aside.

Arrange four noodles in bottom of a 12" Dutch oven or 9" x 12" casserole dish and top with half of the cottage cheese mixture, half of the chicken, and half of the white sauce. Repeat layers, ending with sauce.

Combine bread crumbs, 2 tablespoons parsley, and paprika; sprinkle over casserole.

Bake in Dutch oven for 30 minutes, or in 350°F conventional oven for 30 minutes.

Yield: 6 to 8 servings

TURKEY AND BROWN RICE CASSEROLE

3 cups cooked turkey or chicken, cut in
    large chunks
3½ cups cooked brown rice
1 cup chopped onion
1 cup sliced celery
1 cup chopped green pepper
2 tablespoons plus 1 tablespoon margarine
1 can (10½ ounces) cream of mushroom
    soup
½ cup dry white wine or chicken broth
1 can sliced mushrooms, undrained
1 teaspoon dried sage leaves, crumbled
¼ teaspoon dried thyme leaves
½ teaspoon salt
dash pepper
1 can (4 ounces) pimientos, drained and
    chopped
1 cup herb-seasoned croutons

Combine turkey and rice in Dutch oven or a 2½-quart casserole. Set aside.

Sauté onion, celery, and green pepper in 2 tablespoons of the margarine for 8 minutes, stirring frequently, until tender-crisp. Stir in soup, wine or broth, mushrooms, sage, thyme, salt, pepper, and pimientos. Pour mushroom-vegetable mixture over turkey and rice in casserole or Dutch oven. Stir with large spoon to combine.

Heat remaining 1 tablespoon margarine until melted. Toss croutons in melted margarine. Spoon around edge of Dutch oven. Bake with coals on top and underneath Dutch oven for 35 to 40 minutes, or in 350°F conventional oven for 40 to 45 minutes, until bubbly.

Yield: 8 servings

DAISY TAPPAN RICE DISH

2 cups uncooked brown rice
½ cup butter
1 cup chopped black pitted olives
2 cans (10½ ounces each) chicken broth
4 ounces Cheddar cheese, grated (1 cup)
2 fresh tomatoes, chopped (or 1 can,
    28 ounces)
½ onion, chopped
½ green pepper, seeded and chopped
1 cup water

This recipe is named for Daisy Tappan, who came to the Middle Fork of the Salmon River to live when she was a child of seven. She was every bit as competent in the back country as any man who ever lived there, and spent most of her seventy years there, ranching and raising her family.

Combine all ingredients and mix well.

Bake in Dutch oven for 1 hour, or in 325°F conventional oven for 1½ hours.

Yield: 10 to 12 servings

CHICKEN ENCHILADAS

2 pounds boned, cut-up chicken, cubed
2 tablespoons olive oil
I bunch scallions, diced
I small can (4 ounces) diced green chiles
I can (10 ounces) pitted black olives,
    chopped
2 tablespoons cumin
salt to taste
2 cups sour cream
8 flour tortillas, 7-inch diameter
16 ounces Monterey Jack cheese, grated
    (4 cups)
8 ounces Cheddar cheese, grated (2 cups)
I can (8 ounces) tomato sauce

Brown chicken in oil in Dutch oven or skillet. Add scallions, and continue cooking until scallions are tender. Add chiles, olives, cumin, and salt; mix well. Fold in sour cream.

Cover the bottom of a Dutch oven or 9"x 12" casserole dish with tortillas. Put in a layer of chicken mixture, a layer of the cheeses, and a layer of tomato sauce. Repeat this twice to make three layers. Cover the last layer with tortillas and sprinkle with cheese.

Bake in Dutch oven 40 to 45 minutes, or in 350°F conventional oven for 45 to 50 minutes. Let stand 10 minutes before serving.

Yield: 6 to 8 servings

MOM'S FAMOUS CASSEROLE

Mary Jo Mulick's daughters, Emily and Mattie, named their favorite dinner for her. Mary Jo and husband Jim are longtime friends of ours from Pocatello, Idaho.

12 ounces wide egg noodles, cooked
2 cups diced, cooked chicken or turkey
I can (10½ ounces) cream of chicken
    mushroom soup
2 large bunches of broccoli, cut into
    chunks
4 ounces Cheddar cheese, grated (I cup)
mayonnaise, if needed to moisten

Combine all ingredients in a Dutch oven or 1½-quart casserole dish.

Bake in Dutch oven for 30 to 40 minutes, or in 350°F conventional oven for 40 to 45 minutes.

Yield: 6 servings

ANGIE'S TURKEY CASSEROLE

My sister-in-law, Angie Mills, contributed this recipe.

2 packages (10 ounces each) frozen
    broccoli, thawed and drained
2 cups chopped, cooked turkey
1 can (10½ ounces) cream of chicken
    soup
½ cup mayonnaise
1 tablespoon lemon juice
½ teaspoon curry powder
2 ounces Cheddar cheese, grated (½ cup)
½ cup bread crumbs
2 tablespoons butter, melted

Line a 12" Dutch oven or a 9"x 13" baking pan with broccoli. Top with turkey.

In a separate bowl, mix chicken soup, mayonnaise, lemon juice, and curry powder. Pour over turkey. Mix cheese, bread crumbs, and butter, and sprinkle on top.

Bake in Dutch oven for 25 to 30 minutes, or in 300°F conventional oven for 30 minutes.

Yield: 6 to 8 servings

FISHMONGER TROUT

1 large cucumber, peeled and thinly sliced
1½ teaspoons plus 1½ teaspoons
    chopped fresh dill
1½ teaspoons plus 1 teaspoon fresh
    lemon juice
salt and pepper to taste
1 cup sour cream
1 teaspoon lemon zest
2 trout fillets, 12 to 14 ounces each
2 tablespoons butter, melted

Line a 12" Dutch oven with parchment paper.

Combine cucumber, 1½ teaspoons of the dill, and 1½ teaspoons of the lemon juice. Season with salt and pepper, and set aside.

In a separate bowl, combine sour cream, lemon zest, and remaining lemon juice and stir. Set aside.

Arrange fillets skin side down in Dutch oven or baking dish. Brush with butter. Bake in Dutch oven, or in 350°F conventional oven, until just opaque in center, about 10 minutes.

Divide cucumber mixture among four plates. Place half a trout fillet on top of each serving of cucumbers. Spoon sour cream sauce on top and sprinkle with remaining dill.

Yield: 4 servings

BAKED RAINBOW TROUT

Jerry Myers outfits float trips on the Main Salmon River. He shared this unique recipe with me. Jerry would like you to consider using commercially raised, cold-water trout in order to limit the killing of wild trout.

butter for greasing pan
8 to 12 rainbow trout, cleaned, with or
    without heads and tails (use fillets of
    about 8 ounces each)
2 tablespoons butter
1 cup sliced mushrooms
4 scallions, sliced
2 garlic cloves, minced
2 cups whole wheat cracker crumbs
4 slices bacon, cooked and crumbled
½ teaspoon coarsely ground pepper
½ cup sliced almonds
1 small head of cabbage or lettuce

Grease a 12" Dutch oven or 9"x 12" baking dish and set aside.

Rinse trout and pat dry. Melt butter in a skillet and lightly sauté mushrooms, scallions, and garlic. Mix in cracker crumbs, bacon bits, pepper, and half of the almonds.

With a spoon, stuff about 2 heaping tablespoons of the mixture into each trout. Tear off several leaves of cabbage or lettuce and line the bottom of Dutch oven or dish. Place four stuffed fish on the leaves. Place another layer of leaves, then another layer of fish. Repeat if you are cooking twelve trout. Do *not* cover the top layer with leaves. Sprinkle with the remaining almonds.

Bake in Dutch oven with 6 or 7 charcoals on the bottom and 15 to 20 on top of the oven, 25 to 35 minutes, leaving cover just slightly ajar. If cooking conventionally, cover partially and bake in 375°F conventional oven for 35 to 40 minutes. The cabbage leaves will prevent the fish from sticking to each other or to the pan and add a hearty flavor. Do not overcook.

Yield: 8 to 12 servings

HALIBUT WITH PINEAPPLE SALSA

Pineapple Salsa:

½ cup diced pineapple
½ cup diced red bell pepper
¼ cup chopped cilantro
2 teaspoons minced jalapeño pepper
⅛ teaspoon salt
¼ cup fresh lime juice
I teaspoon canola oil

Halibut:

oil for greasing grill racks
I teaspoon canola oil
4 halibut steaks, 4 ounces each (about
    I inch thick)
⅛ teaspoon salt
lime wedges for garnish

Grease grill racks liberally.

Make the salsa: Combine pineapple, red pepper, cilantro, jalapeño, salt, lime juice, and oil. Stir well. Let stand 15 minutes, stirring occasionally.

Brush fish with 1 teaspoon oil and sprinkle with salt. Set aside.

Place fish on grill rack and cook 5 minutes on each side or until fish flakes easily with a fork. Serve with pineapple salsa and lime wedges.

Yield: 4 servings

SWORDFISH WITH MUSTARD SAUCE

½ teaspoon finely chopped shallots
3 tablespoons dry white wine
I cup whipping cream
I ½ tablespoons Dijon mustard
salt and pepper to taste
4 swordfish fillets, 6 ounces each

Combine shallots and wine in a saucepan. Bring to a boil, then simmer until the wine is reduced by one-third. Blend in whipping cream and mustard. Season with salt and pepper to taste.

Grill the swordfish until it is browned on both sides and the flesh flakes easily with a fork. Spoon mustard sauce over the fish to serve.

Yield: 4 servings

STEAMED FISH WITH BLACK BEAN SAUCE

4 sea bass or other firm fish (about
    2 pounds total)
1 piece (1 inch long) fresh ginger root,
    peeled
4 tablespoons Chinese sesame oil
¼ cup plus 2 teaspoons soy sauce
2 scallions, cut into 1-inch pieces and
    slivered
½ cup canned black beans
1 tablespoon sherry (optional)

Wash the fish and pat dry with paper towel. Place in a large bowl.

Slice the ginger root into 12 thin slices, and then sliver. Combine sesame oil, ¼ cup of the soy sauce, ¾ of the slivered ginger root, and scallions. Pour over fish.

Rinse black beans twice in warm water and drain well.

In a separate bowl, mince remainder of ginger root. Add beans and crush together. Add remaining 2 teaspoons soy sauce and the sherry, if desired. Rub mixture over fish.

Fill Dutch oven or 2-quart casserole dish 2 inches deep with water. Place fish in a shallow bowl or on a rack over water and bring water to a simmer.

Cook until the fish is done and flakes with a fork, 10 to 15 minutes in Dutch oven, or 20 to 25 minutes in 350°F conventional oven.

Yield: 4 servings

FLORENTINED SOLE

3 packages (10 ounces each) frozen
    spinach, thawed and drained
1 cup plus 1 cup sour cream
¼ cup chopped scallions
4 pounds sole fillets
salt and pepper to taste
6 slices uncooked bacon
4 tablespoons dried parsley
paprika to taste (optional)

Combine spinach, 1 cup of the sour cream, and scallions in a bowl and mix well. Spread the mixture on the bottom of the Dutch oven and place the sole fillets on top. Salt and pepper well. Spread remainder of sour cream on fillets and lay slices of bacon on top. Sprinkle with parsley and paprika, if desired.

Bake in Dutch oven for 30 to 40 minutes, or in 350°F conventional oven for 30 to 40 minutes.

Yield: 8 to 10 servings

SCALLADOS

1 pound fresh or frozen scallops
3 medium avocados, halved, pitted, and peeled
2 tablespoons fresh lemon juice
¾ cup dry white wine
¼ cup minced scallions
1 cup sliced fresh mushrooms
½ teaspoon salt
pepper to taste
3 tablespoons margarine
4 tablespoons unbleached all-purpose flour
¾ cup milk
2 ounces Swiss cheese, grated (½ cup)

Thaw scallops, if frozen. Brush avocados with lemon juice and set aside. Place the scallops in a Dutch oven or saucepan and add wine, scallions, mushrooms, salt, and pepper. Bring to a simmer, cover, and simmer very slowly for 5 minutes.

With a slotted spoon, remove scallops, mushrooms, and onions to a bowl. Reserve liquid in a separate dish.

Melt margarine in Dutch oven. Stir in the flour and cook slowly for 2 minutes without browning. Remove from heat and beat in the scallop liquid slowly, stirring until the sauce thickens. Thin out with milk. Carefully correct seasoning, adding more lemon juice if needed.

Fold two-thirds of the sauce into the scallop mixture and spoon into avocado halves. Add cheese to the remaining sauce and stir until cheese melts. Spoon the remaining sauce over avocados.

Heat in covered Dutch oven to bubbling with heat on the top only. In a conventional oven, broil until sauce is bubbling.

Yield: 6 servings

SEAFOOD THERMIDOR

If you think that lobster Thermidor is the ultimate in good eating but you shudder at the cost, here's a delicious entree made in the same style but with cod, the "poor man's lobster."

oil for greasing pan
1 pound fresh or frozen cod fillets
1 small onion, quartered
1 lemon slice
1 can (10½ ounces) cream of shrimp soup
3 tablespoons unbleached all-purpose flour
¼ cup milk
¼ cup dry white wine
1 ounce mozzarella cheese, grated (¼ cup)
2 tablespoons snipped fresh parsley
½ cup soft bread crumbs
2 tablespoons grated Parmesan cheese
2 tablespoons margarine
½ teaspoon paprika

Lightly grease a skillet or Dutch oven and set aside.

Thaw cod if frozen, and skin if necessary. Cut into ½-inch cubes. Place cod, onion, and lemon slice in skillet or Dutch oven. Add water to cover. Bring to boil, reduce heat, and simmer, covered, for 5 to 6 minutes or until fish flakes easily. Carefully drain fish well.

In a small saucepan, blend shrimp soup and flour. Gradually stir in milk and wine. Cook and stir until thickened and bubbly. Stir in mozzarella and parsley. Heat through. Fold fish into sauce. Spoon into four scallop shells or onto plates. If cooking in Dutch oven, place filled shells in bottom.

Combine bread crumbs, Parmesan, margarine, and paprika. Sprinkle over sauce.

Heat in covered Dutch oven to bubbling with heat on the top only, or broil in conventional oven 1 to 2 minutes, until cheese melts.

Yield: 4 servings

THALWEG STRUDEL

This is the most asked-for recipe on the Rocky Mountain River Tours menu. We named it for a "thalweg," the deepest, fastest-moving channel in a river.

16 phyllo dough leaves
½ pound (2 sticks) unsalted butter, melted
1 pound scallops
6 ounces crab meat
1 pound fresh mushrooms, sliced
5 scallions, chopped
16 ounces cream cheese, softened
1 egg white
32 stalks fresh asparagus
2 cups Hollandaise sauce (prepare a purchased sauce or make Jiffy Hollandaise, page 72)

For each of 8 strudels, lay out one of the phyllo leaves and brush with melted butter. Top with another leaf and brush that with butter also.

Mix scallops, crab meat, mushrooms, scallions, and cream cheese in a large bowl and place about 1 cup of the mixture at the end of the phyllo leaves. Roll up, fold the sides over, and continue to roll. Place on baking sheet or in Dutch oven with open edge down. Do this with each strudel and brush them with egg white.

Bake in Dutch oven for 30 minutes, or in 375°F conventional oven for 30 to 40 minutes, or until golden brown.

Cut woody ends off asparagus, and steam stalks.

Prepare Hollandaise sauce. Garnish each strudel with asparagus and top with Hollandaise.

Yield: 8 servings

SPAGHETTI SQUASH WITH SHRIMP SAUCE

1 spaghetti squash (about 2 pounds), cut
    in half lengthwise and seeded
1 tablespoon butter
1 large garlic clove, minced
1 medium-sized red bell pepper, seeded
    and cut in ¼-inch strips
1 medium-sized zucchini, cut in ¼-inch strips
1 cup dry white wine
1 teaspoon dried basil
hot pepper sauce to taste
salt to taste
freshly ground pepper to taste
12 ounces cooked peeled shrimp, chopped
chopped fresh parsley for garnish
grated Parmesan cheese for garnish

Steam squash over boiling water for about 30 minutes. Using a fork, separate squash strands. Remove from heat and keep warm.

Melt butter in skillet and add garlic, red bell pepper, and zucchini. Toss to coat. Sauté about 5 minutes or until vegetables are softened. Add wine and basil. Season with hot pepper sauce, salt, and pepper, and bring to a boil. Add shrimp and cook until heated through.

Pour sauce over squash and toss to combine. Sprinkle with fresh parsley and serve with Parmesan cheese.

Yield: 4 servings

STUFFED SCAMPI

12 large shrimp, peeled and cleaned
1 onion, chopped
2 cups chopped celery
½ cup unsalted butter
12 ounces tiny shrimp
¼ teaspoon minced garlic
¼ teaspoon dried thyme
1 tablespoon chopped fresh parsley
1 tablespoon tomato sauce
3 tablespoons white wine
4 ounces Parmesan cheese, grated (1 cup)
1 cup dried bread crumbs
2 tablespoons butter, melted

Butterfly the shrimp by cutting in half lengthwise, but *don't cut all the way through.*

Sauté onion and celery in butter until onion is golden. Add the tiny shrimp and sauté 5 to 7 minutes, until just cooked. Remove from heat. Add garlic, thyme, parsley, tomato sauce, wine, and Parmesan cheese. Mix until blended. Add bread crumbs and sauté another 3 minutes. Cool.

Arrange the shrimp, cut side up, in a Dutch oven or 2-quart casserole dish. Pile stuffing on each shrimp to cover completely. Brush with melted butter.

Bake in Dutch oven for 10 to 15 minutes, or in 350°F conventional oven for 10 to 15 minutes, or until shrimp are cooked through.

Yield: 4 to 6 servings

SHRIMP QUICHE

pastry for 10" single-crust pie (recipe on
    page 143
1 can (5½ ounces) whole shrimp, well
    drained
⅓ cup chopped scallions (tops included)
4 ounces Swiss cheese, grated (1 cup)
3 eggs
1 cup milk
½ teaspoon salt
⅛ teaspoon pepper

Prepare the pastry recipe, or a pie crust mix.

Line the bottom of Dutch oven or 9" pie dish with the pastry shell. Distribute shrimp over the bottom of pastry. Sprinkle evenly with the scallions and cheese.

In a separate bowl, beat together the eggs, milk, salt, and pepper. Pour over shrimp and cheese.

Bake in Dutch oven for 35 to 40 minutes, or in 350°F oven for about 45 minutes, or until custard is firm in the center. Let stand for 10 minutes before serving.

Yield: 6 to 8 servings

CARIBBEAN BEANS AND GRILLED THAI SHRIMP

1 jar (12 ounces) Thai peanut sauce
    (available at Asian markets)
24 large, fresh shrimp, peeled and cleaned
2 medium yellow onions, chopped
4 garlic cloves, crushed
1 tablespoon olive oil
2 cans red beans, drained
2 cans black beans, drained
1 small jar (8 ounces) tomatillo salsa
1 cup chopped cilantro
8 flour tortillas, 7-inch diameter

Pour peanut sauce over shrimp and marinate in refrigerator for 2 hours or overnight.

Sauté onions and garlic in oil until soft. Add beans. Cook until heated through. Mash partially. Add salsa and cilantro. Spread over tortillas and roll up.

Put shrimp on skewers and grill for 5 minutes on outdoor grill. Serve with bean tortillas and Papaya Salsa (recipe on page 66).

Yield: 8 servings

FETA SHRIMP BAKE

This is always a favorite dish on Rocky Mountain River Tours' Middle Fork float trips.

1¼ cups chopped onion
4 garlic cloves, minced
⅛ cup olive oil
6 fresh tomatoes, chopped
½ cup chopped fresh parsley
1 tablespoon chopped fresh basil
2 teaspoons fresh marjoram
2 teaspoons grated lemon peel
salt and freshly ground pepper to taste
1 teaspoon allspice
3 pounds shrimp, peeled and cleaned
1½ pounds feta cheese, crumbled
1 pound linguini pasta, cooked

In a Dutch oven or skillet, sauté onion and garlic in oil. Add tomatoes, parsley, basil, marjoram, and lemon peel. Simmer about 10 minutes. Season with salt, pepper, and allspice. If preparing conventionally, pour mixture into 2-quart casserole dish.

Put the shrimp on top of mixture. Sprinkle with feta cheese.

Bake in Dutch oven for about 20 minutes, or in 350°F conventional oven for 30 to 40 minutes, until the shrimp is done. Serve on top of linguini.

Yield: 8 servings

SALMON RIVER LASAGNA

This is an easy salmon recipe from my sister, Marcia Colliat. It adapts very well to a Dutch oven.

1 can (7½ ounces) salmon, drained
1 cup ricotta cheese
6 ounces Parmesan cheese, grated (1½ cups, divided)
4 ounces cream cheese
1 egg
1 pound fresh spfoglia pasta sheets, uncooked (or 6 cooked and drained lasagna noodles)
6 ounces mozzarella cheese, grated (1½ cups)
1 cup spaghetti sauce (your favorite)
½ package (5 ounces) frozen spinach, thawed and drained

Remove any skin and bones from the salmon and flake.

Mix ricotta cheese, ½ cup of the Parmesan, cream cheese, and egg.

If using spfoglia, slice the sheets of pasta lengthwise into thirds. Line the bottom of a 12" Dutch oven or 9"x 12" baking dish with a layer of pasta. Top with half of the cheese mixture, half of the salmon, ½ cup of the mozzarella cheese, half of the spaghetti sauce, and half of the spinach. Place another layer of pasta over the top, and repeat other layers.

Bake in Dutch oven for 20 to 30 minutes, or in 350°F conventional oven for 35 to 45 minutes.

Sprinkle with remaining ½ cup mozzarella and 1 cup Parmesan. Bake 5 more minutes. Let stand for a few minutes before slicing.

Yield: 8 servings

SALMON SOUFFLÉ

butter for greasing pan
3 tablespoons butter
3 tablespoons unbleached all-purpose
    flour
1 teaspoon salt
dash freshly ground pepper
1 cup milk
1 can (16 ounces) salmon, drained and
    flaked
2 tablespoons lemon juice
1 tablespoon grated onion
3 tablespoons chopped fresh parsley
3 eggs, separated

Butter a Dutch oven or 1½-quart casserole dish.

Melt butter in a skillet and blend in flour, salt, and pepper. Gradually add milk and cook on low heat, stirring all the while, until thickened. Add salmon, lemon juice, onion, and parsley.

In a separate bowl, beat egg yolks until thick and lemon-colored. Gradually stir eggs into salmon mixture. Mix well.

Beat egg whites until stiff and fold gently into salmon mixture. Turn into Dutch oven or casserole dish.

Bake in Dutch oven for about 35 to 40 minutes, or in 375°F conventional oven for about 50 minutes.

Yield: 6 servings

SALMON CHEESE CASSEROLE

1 can (16 ounces) salmon, with liquid
1 can (4 ounces) mushrooms, drained and
    sliced, or 4 ounces fresh
1½ cups bread crumbs
2 eggs, beaten
4 ounces Cheddar cheese, grated (1 cup)
1 tablespoon lemon juice
1 tablespoon minced onion

Flake fish in a bowl, removing all bones. Add all remaining ingredients and mix thoroughly. Pour into Dutch oven or 1½-quart casserole dish.

Bake in Dutch oven for 30 to 35 minutes, or in 350°F conventional oven for 35 to 40 minutes.

Yield: 6 servings

MEAT DISHES

REMEMBER

When a recipe calls for baking, braising, stewing, or roasting, the Dutch oven must be covered with charcoal briquettes on top of the lid. For boiling, frying, sautéing, and quick-heating, leave the Dutch oven cover off. For more on cooking techniques for the Dutch oven, see "Dutch Oven Care and Use," pages 2–3.

ESPECIAL DEL RIO DE HOMBRE POBRE

"The poor man's river special" was devised by Gregg Tipton for a fishing trip down the Green River in Utah a few years ago. Its ease of preparation was an instant hit with all Gregg's cohorts, since their main task of the evening was chasing Mr. Wily Trout!

Guacamole:

4 ripe, large avocados
1 cup chopped scallions
2 cups chopped cilantro
2 tomatoes, chopped
1 jar (10 ounces) picante sauce
3 tablespoons garlic powder
1 tablespoon pepper
juice of 1 lemon
1 head of lettuce, shredded, for garnish

Assembly:

2 pounds pork, beef or chicken, cut into
    1/2-inch chunks (may use hamburger)
1 red onion, chopped
1 can (4 ounce) diced jalapeños (use less
    for medium heat)
24 corn tortillas, 8-inch diameter
2 bell peppers, seeded and chopped
2 tomatoes, chopped
16 ounces Cheddar cheese, grated
    (4 cups)

Make the guacamole: Peel and pit avocados. Mash in large bowl. Add scallions, cilantro, and two chopped tomatoes. Add picante sauce to taste, garlic powder, pepper, and lemon juice. Mix well. Cover and keep cool until ready to serve.

Sauté the meat. After 3 to 5 minutes add one third of the chopped red onion and the jalapeños. Cook until meat is rare.

In a circular pattern layer bottom of a 12" Dutch oven or 2-quart casserole dish with eight to twelve of the tortillas, with edges of tortillas coming two to three inches up the sides of dish. Add meat mixture, spreading evenly. Add another layer of four to six tortillas placed up to the edges of the dish. Add peppers, two chopped tomatoes, and the rest of the onion. Spread evenly. Cover with eight or so more tortillas.

Bake in Dutch oven for 20 minutes, or cover and bake in 350°F conventional oven for 20 minutes. Sprinkle with cheese and bake another 5 to 10 minutes.

Cut in wedges and serve topped with lettuce and guacamole.

Yield: 6 to 8 servings

BETTY'S BEEF AND POTATO BAKE

Thanks to my sister-in-law, Betty Mills, from Coeur d'Alene, Idaho, for contributing this recipe.

4 cups peeled, thinly sliced potatoes
1 cup plus ¼ cup chopped yellow onion
1 teaspoon salt
⅛ teaspoon plus 1 teaspoon pepper
1 teaspoon parsley flakes
1 pound ground beef
¾ cup milk
½ cup rolled oats
¼ cup tomato sauce

Arrange potatoes, 1 cup of the chopped onion, salt, ⅛ teaspoon pepper, and parsley flakes evenly in Dutch oven or loaf pan.

In a separate bowl, mix ground beef, milk, oats, tomato sauce, ¼ cup onion, and 1 teaspoon pepper. Pour over potato mixture in Dutch oven or pan.

Bake in Dutch oven for 25 to 30 minutes, or in 350°F conventional oven for 30 to 40 minutes.

Yield: 4 servings

BUNCE'S CHICKEN AND CHOPS

Mike Bunce created this sweet-and-sour dish, which has become a favorite among his river buddies. He likes to cook it long and slowly so that everything falls apart.

6 tablespoons olive oil
12 pork chops, trimmed of fat
12 chicken thighs, skinned
12 chicken breasts, skinned
lots of coarsely ground pepper
1 teaspoon garlic powder
1 can (15 ounces) Contadina sweet-and-sour sauce
1 large onion, chopped
2 green peppers, seeded and chopped
4 ounces mushrooms, chopped

Heat oil in Dutch oven or large skillet. Brown pork chops and chicken with pepper and garlic powder (may have to do in batches). Layer in large Dutch oven or 2-quart casserole dish and pour sweet and sour sauce over the top. Add onion, green peppers, and mushrooms.

Bake in Dutch oven with mostly top heat for 40 to 50 minutes, or cover and bake in 350°F conventional oven for 45 to 50 minutes, or until meat falls off the bones.

Yield: 15 servings

BOOMER'S SALMON RIVER MEAT ROLLS

Werner Rosenbaum's mother gave him the recipe for this popular German dish. It is the highlight of his river trips and is in such demand that he is asked to prepare it ahead for groups that go down the river when he is not even on the trip! It is very inexpensive and easy to prepare, and feeds a lot of people. Serve with boiled or fried potatoes.

1 or 2 pieces top round steak (4 pounds total), sliced ⅛-inch thick per serving
salt and pepper
2 onions, chopped
2 slices uncooked bacon per serving
4 dill pickles, sliced (optional)
olive oil for browning meat
2 tablespoons cornstarch

Lay round steak out flat. Lightly salt and pepper top only. Sprinkle with half the chopped onions and lay bacon on top. Roll up steak and secure with a heavy toothpick. (Variation: A slice of dill pickle can also be rolled up inside steak.) Brown meat in bacon grease or olive oil.

Put meat rolls in large Dutch oven or skillet and cover with water. Add any remaining onions. Simmer 1½ hours. Remove meat and thicken gravy with cornstarch. Put meat back in gravy.

This dish can be prepared ahead of time, frozen, and reheated in the Dutch oven.

Yield: 18 to 20 servings

PEGGY'S LAMB

This is the main dish that won the 1988 World Championship Dutch Oven Cookoff, a major event of the Festival of the American West in Logan, Utah. It was prepared by Rosemary Parkinson and Peggy Roskelley of Smithfield, Utah.

1 garlic clove
2 teaspoons fresh marjoram
½ teaspoon salt
2 tablespoons lemon juice
½ teaspoon Tabasco
leg of lamb, 3 to 4 pounds
20 small pimiento-stuffed green olives
2 strips uncooked bacon, cut in ½-inch pieces

Mash and mix together garlic, marjoram, and salt. Add lemon juice and Tabasco.

Make 10 holes in lamb leg with sharp narrow knife, as far as you can cut without cutting through the meat. Push a green olive in each hole, then a piece of bacon, ½ teaspoon of the garlic mixture, then another stuffed olive. Repeat until all holes are filled.

For Dutch oven cooking, roast in 12" Dutch oven with about ten coals underneath and eighteen around the rim of the top, for 3 hours. For conventional cooking, bake in covered 2-quart casserole dish in 350°F conventional oven for 3 hours. Garnish with parsley, or serve with stir-fried vegetables heaped around the meat.

Yield: 8 servings

SHIITAKE LASAGNA

butter for greasing pan
1 ounce dried shiitake mushrooms
2 cups warm water
2 pounds fresh mushrooms, finely
    chopped
¼ cup olive oil
¼ cup plus ½ cup unsalted butter
1 medium-sized onion, finely chopped
1 can (14 ounces) Italian plum tomatoes,
    drained and chopped (can use fresh)
½ cup chopped fresh parsley
⅓ cup unbleached all-purpose flour
2 cups milk
1 teaspoon nutmeg
dash of salt
1 pound fresh spfoglia pasta sheets, un-
    cooked (or 6 cooked and drained
    lasagna noodles)
6 ounces prosciutto, thinly sliced
8 ounces Parmesan cheese, grated
    (2 cups)
paprika and ground black pepper to taste

Butter a 12" Dutch oven.

Stem the shiitake mushrooms and soak for at least 30 minutes in warm water. Reserving the water, remove mushrooms and chop them.

Cook fresh mushrooms in olive oil and ¼ cup of the butter until liquid is reduced to almost nothing. Add the shiitake mushrooms, onion, tomatoes, and parsley. Cook for 15 minutes, partially covered.

To make the sauce, melt remaining ½ cup butter and add flour gradually. Stir 5 minutes over low heat. Slowly stir in milk and liquid from shiitake mushrooms. Cook until thickened and smooth, about 10 to 12 minutes. Add nutmeg and salt. Strain shiitake liquid through a sieve lined with paper towels.

If using spfoglia, cut each sheet of pasta lengthwise into three strips. Place in bottom of Dutch oven or 9"x 12" baking pan, slightly overlapping strips. Layer with mushroom mixture, sauce, and prosciutto. Sprinkle with Parmesan. Top should be covered with one last layer of pasta and topped with rest of sauce and cheese. Sprinkle with paprika and pepper.

Bake in Dutch oven for 20 to 25 minutes, or bake uncovered in 350°F conventional oven for 35 to 45 minutes. Lasagna should be golden brown on top. Let stand ten minutes before serving.

Yield: 10 to 12 servings

MOROCCAN COUSCOUS OF LAMB, FRUIT, AND VEGETABLES

⅔ cup uncooked couscous
⅔ cup dried currants
½ cup chicken stock
¼ cup olive oil
10 ounces lean boneless lamb, cut into
    1-inch cubes
4 large garlic cloves, minced
salt to taste
1 apple, peeled, cored, and cut into
    6 pieces
1 red bell pepper, seeded and cut into
    1-inch pieces
6 medium scallions, cut into thirds
6 carrots, peeled and cut into 1-inch
    lengths
¼ cup pine nuts
2 teaspoons fresh lemon juice
1 teaspoon cinnamon
¼ teaspoon cayenne pepper

Place couscous and currants in small bowl. Bring chicken stock to a boil and pour over couscous and currants. Stir with fork, cover bowl, and set aside.

Heat olive oil in Dutch oven. Sauté and stir lamb, garlic, and salt in oil. Reduce heat and add apple, bell pepper, scallions, and carrots. Cover and cook until lamb is no longer pink.

Add pine nuts, lemon juice, cinnamon, and cayenne, tossing gently to blend. Cover and cook until just heated through. Adjust seasoning and serve over couscous.

Yield: 6 servings

SALMON RIVER STEW

2 pounds beef chuck, cut in 1½-inch cubes
1 pound ground pork sausage
2 cups hot water
1 garlic clove
3 medium onions, sliced
2 bay leaves
1 tablespoon salt
2 teaspoons pepper
6 carrots, sliced
4 potatoes, cubed
2 green peppers, seeded and chopped
6 fresh tomatoes, cubed
8 ounces Cheddar cheese, grated (2 cups)

Brown beef and sausage in a skillet or Dutch oven. Drain well. Add hot water, garlic, onions, bay leaves, salt, pepper, carrots, potatoes, green peppers, and tomatoes.

Cover and simmer for 45 to 50 minutes, stirring occasionally to keep from sticking. Remove bay leaves and garlic clove.

Cook another 10 minutes or until vegetables are tender. Sprinkle cheese on top and cover; heat until cheese melts.

Yield: 8 to 10 servings

CHEF'S HATS

6 frozen puff pastry shells
6 ounces Cheddar cheese, grated
    (1½ cups)
3 tablespoons unbleached all-purpose
    flour
3 eggs, lightly beaten
1 package (10 ounces) frozen chopped
    spinach, thawed and drained
4 ounces fresh mushrooms, sliced
6 crisply cooked bacon slices, crumbled
½ teaspoon salt
dash pepper

Roll out each pastry shell into a 6- to 8-inch circle. Line paper muffin cups with each circle of dough, so that edges of dough stand up at least a half-inch above the cup edge.

Toss cheese with flour. Add eggs, spinach, mushrooms, bacon, salt, and pepper. Mix well. Fill the cups with cheese mixture.

Bake in Dutch oven for 25 to 30 minutes, or in 350°F conventional oven for 40 minutes.

Yield: 6 servings

BOEUF BOURGUIGNONNE

6 strips uncooked bacon, cut in ½-inch
    pieces
3 pounds beef rump or chuck, cut in
    1½-inch cubes
1 large carrot, peeled and sliced
1 medium onion, sliced
1½ teaspoons salt
⅛ teaspoon pepper
3 tablespoons unbleached all-purpose
    flour
1 can (10½ ounces) condensed beef
    broth
1½ cups red wine
1 teaspoon tomato paste
4 garlic cloves, minced
1½ teaspoons thyme
1 bay leaf
8 ounces small white onions, peeled
1 pound fresh mushrooms, sliced
2 tablespoons margarine

Cook bacon in Dutch oven or skillet until crisp. Remove bacon. Add beef cubes and brown well in the bacon fat. Remove browned beef and set aside. Brown carrot and onion. Season with salt and pepper. Stir in flour. Add broth and mix well.

Put beef back in Dutch oven, or place all in 2-quart casserole dish. Add cooked bacon, wine, tomato paste, garlic, thyme, bay leaf, and onions.

Bake in Dutch oven for 45 minutes on medium heat, or cover and bake in 350°F conventional oven for 45 minutes.

Meanwhile, sauté mushrooms in margarine. Add mushrooms to Dutch oven or casserole; cook 15 more minutes.

Yield: 6 to 8 servings

CLAIR'S DUTCH OVEN ENCHILADAS

Clair Yost, who gave me this special recipe, has been boating for fun and profit for a number of years. He has a special knack for cooking in a Dutch oven.

2 pounds ground beef
I onion, diced
I green bell pepper, seeded and diced
seasoned salt to taste
I ½ tablespoons plus 4 tablespoons
    ground cumin
ground black pepper to taste
I can (29 ounces) tomato sauce
I can (12 ounces) tomato paste
I can (10 ounces) enchilada sauce
    (medium-hot)
I dozen corn tortillas, 8-inch diameter
10 fresh mushrooms, sliced
I medium ripe avocado, peeled, pitted, and
    diced
3 fresh tomatoes, cut into 8 sections each
2 pounds sharp Cheddar cheese, grated
    (8 cups)
I head lettuce
sour cream and hot sauce for garnish

Variations: You can replace the ground beef with chopped and browned round steak. To make this dish vegetarian, replace beef with brown rice held together with mozzarella cheese and seasoned with cumin. Or, make an enchilada pie with the same ingredients, in four layers, using three tortillas cut into fourths to start each layer. Bake the same way in a Dutch oven or casserole.

Brown the beef with onion and green pepper. Pour off grease. Season to taste with seasoned salt, 1½ tablespoons cumin, and pepper

In a separate pan, heat tomato sauce, tomato paste, enchilada sauce, and remaining 4 tablespoons cumin. Simmer for 5 minutes.

Dip each tortilla into the heated sauce to make it soft. Lay each tortilla on a plate and spread beef mixture across the middle of each. Put several mushrooms, avocado pieces, two tomato sections, and grated cheese on top of beef for each tortilla. Roll up tortillas to make enchiladas. Place six rolled enchiladas in a 12" Dutch oven or 9"x 12" baking dish, fold side down.

Pour some sauce over top of enchiladas; spread cheese over sauce. Repeat process with remaining six tortillas, and stack on top of others. Put any remaining meat mixture, vegetables, and cheese on top. Cover.

For Dutch oven cooking, line the outside of the lid with charcoal briquettes, place four briquettes in the center, and place eight briquettes on the bottom. Bake 30 minutes, checking center and making sure the heat is not too hot. Bake 15 to 20 minutes more. Take coals off and let stand 10 minutes before serving.

For conventional cooking, bake uncovered in 350°F oven for 45 to 50 minutes.

Serve enchiladas on beds of lettuce leaves. Top with sour cream and hot sauce.

Yield: 6 to 8 servings

NICKY'S LASAGNA

Bill Caccia gave me this recipe, which we made part of the menu on our Main Salmon River float trips.

1 pound ground beef
1 onion, minced
6 cups cottage cheese
10 lasagna noodles, cooked al dente
1 large can (28 ounces) tomato sauce
1 small can (6 ounces) tomato paste
2 teaspoons dried sweet basil
2 teaspoons dried oregano
½ cup red wine
1 pound mozzarella cheese, sliced or
    grated (4 cups)
8 ounces mushrooms, sliced
grated Parmesan cheese for garnish

Variation: To make this dish vegetarian, substitute raw zucchini for the beef. Sauté the onions in a little olive oil.

Brown the ground beef and onion in skillet or Dutch oven. Drain off fat.

Place half of beef-onion mixture in bottom of Dutch oven or 9"x 12" baking dish. Spread half the cottage cheese over beef. Cover with half the lasagna noodles. Cover noodles with half the tomato sauce and half the tomato paste. Sprinkle with sweet basil and oregano and ¼ cup of the wine. Repeat the layer.

Bake in Dutch oven for 30 to 35 minutes, or in 350°F conventional oven for 35 to 40 minutes. Sprinkle with mozzarella cheese and cover with mushrooms. Bake 10 more minutes (if baking in conventional oven, leave cover off for last 10 minutes). Serve with Parmesan cheese.

Yield: 6 to 8 servings

PORK'S COMPANION

This is a favorite recipe of my good friend, Jim Mulick, who's been floating rivers with me for years. Jim's meat loaf is as spicy as his personality, and he feels the secret ingredient is the pork.

1½ pounds ground beef
8 ounces ground pork
2 eggs, beaten
½ cup wheat germ
½ cup bread cubes
1 can (8 ounces) tomato sauce
¼ cup finely chopped onion
¼ cup chopped green pepper
¼ cup chopped celery
1 tablespoon Worcestershire sauce
dash dried thyme, crushed
½ teaspoon dried oregano
½ teaspoon dried sage
1 teaspoon salt

Combine all ingredients and mix well. Shape mixture into a loaf and place in Dutch oven or 9"x 9" baking dish.

Bake in Dutch oven for 1 hour at moderate heat, or in 350°F conventional oven for about 1¼ hours.

Yield: 6 to 8 servings

PORK CHOPS WITH SPINACH DUMPLINGS

6 rib, sirloin, or blade pork chops
salt and pepper to taste
½ cup chopped onion
I garlic clove, minced
1¾ cups plus ¼ cup tomato juice
I can (8 ounces) mushroom stems and
    pieces, drained
I teaspoon sugar
½ teaspoon salt
dash pepper
¼ teaspoon dried thyme, crushed
¼ teaspoon dried marjoram, crushed
¼ teaspoon dried rosemary, crushed
I beaten egg
I package (10 ounces) frozen chopped
    spinach, thawed and drained
⅓ cup fine dry bread crumbs or wheat
    germ
I ounce Parmesan cheese, grated (¼ cup)
I tablespoon butter, melted
2 tablespoons unbleached all-purpose
    flour

Trim excess fat from chops. Cook fat trimmings in Dutch oven or skillet until 2 tablespoons drippings accumulate. Discard fat pieces. Season chops with salt and pepper and brown in hot drippings. Remove chops and set aside.

In the same Dutch oven or skillet, cook onion and garlic until onion is tender but not brown. Add 1¾ cups of the tomato juice, mushrooms, sugar, salt, pepper, thyme, marjoram, and rosemary. Return chops to pan. Simmer, covered, for 20 to 25 minutes.

Meanwhile, combine egg, spinach, bread crumbs, Parmesan, and butter in a separate bowl. Place 2 tablespoons of spinach mixture atop each chop to form a dumpling. Simmer, covered, until dumplings are heated through, 10 to 15 minutes. Place chops and dumplings on a platter.

In a small bowl, blend flour with the remaining ¼ cup tomato juice. Stir into pan juices. Cook and stir until thickened and bubbly. Pour sauce over chops.

Yield: 6 servings

SAUSAGE-STUFFED ACORN SQUASH

2 large acorn squash, cut in half
salt to season squash
1 pound bulk pork sausage
1 cup chopped celery
½ cup sliced fresh mushrooms
¼ cup chopped onion
1 egg, slightly beaten
½ cup sour cream
1 ounce Parmesan cheese, grated (¼ cup)
¼ teaspoon salt

Scoop the seeds out of the four halves of squash. Lightly salt inside of each squash. Place squash in Dutch oven or 9"x 12" baking pan. Bake in Dutch oven for about 25 to 30 minutes, or in 350°F conventional oven for 30 minutes, until tender.

Combine sausage, celery, mushrooms, and onion in skillet. Sauté until vegetables are tender and meat is brown. Drain well.

Combine egg, sour cream, Parmesan, and ¼ teaspoon salt in a separate bowl. Stir into sausage mixture. Fill each squash half with sausage mixture and place halves in Dutch oven or 2-quart casserole dish.

Bake in Dutch oven for 15 to 20 minutes, or cover and bake in 350°F conventional oven for 20 minutes.

Yield: 4 to 6 servings

STUFFED PORK CHOPS

Stuffing:

1 tablespoon margarine
6 fresh mushrooms, sliced
½ cup sliced scallions
¾ cup cooked brown rice
1 tablespoon soy sauce
¼ teaspoon ground ginger

Pork Chops:

6 large pork chops, 1 inch thick
3 tablespoons unbleached all-purpose
    flour
¼ teaspoon garlic salt
¼ teaspoon dry mustard
 pepper to taste
1 egg, lightly beaten
⅓ cup fine bread crumbs
3 tablespoons margarine

Make the stuffing: Melt 1 tablespoon margarine. Add the mushrooms and cook until tender. Add the scallions and rice. Stir in soy sauce and ginger. Remove from heat.

Trim the fat from the pork chops and cut a pocket in the side of each. Stuff each pocket with about 3 tablespoons of the filling. Secure pockets with skewers or toothpicks.

Combine the flour, garlic salt, mustard, and pepper. Dredge each chop in the flour mixture to coat all sides. Dip in egg, then in bread crumbs.

Melt 3 tablespoons margarine in a skillet. Add the chops and cook over low heat until brown on all sides, about 40 to 45 minutes, turning over halfway through cooking time.

Yield: 6 servings

SWEET STEAK

My aunt, Mac Oliver, gave me this recipe. She usually serves it with buttered noodles. This recipe was a winner about ten years ago in a Montana Cowbelles beef cook-off.

2 pounds round steak, cut in serving-sized pieces
1 cup unbleached all-purpose flour for dredging
2 tablespoons olive oil
salt to taste
pepper to taste
½ cup minced onion
1 cup brown sugar
1 can (7¾ ounces) tomato sauce
1 can (10½ ounces) pizza sauce
2 cups water
2 tablespoons parsley flakes
flour or cornstarch for thickening (optional)

Pound steak until tender. Dredge each piece in flour and brown in oil in Dutch oven or skillet. Salt and pepper to taste. If cooking conventionally, move steak to 2-quart casserole dish.

In a separate bowl, mix onion, brown sugar, tomato sauce, pizza sauce, water, and parsley flakes. Pour sauce over steak.

Simmer slowly in Dutch oven for about 1½ hours, or cook covered in 325°F conventional oven for 1½ hours. If necessary, add flour or cornstarch to thicken gravy.

Yield: 6 servings

WITCHES' BREW

1 pound uncooked bacon
1 pound hamburger
1 cup diced celery
1 cup diced onion
1 can (28 ounces) tomatoes
2 cans red kidney beans
1 can mushrooms
1 cup egg noodles, uncooked

Fry bacon and hamburger in Dutch oven or large skillet. Drain off fat. Add celery, onion, tomatoes, beans, mushrooms, and noodles.

Bake 45 minutes in Dutch oven, or 1 hour in 350°F conventional oven.

Yield: 8 to 10 servings

TAMALE PIE

This is also good served cold on lettuce leaves, similar to a taco salad.

1 medium onion, chopped
1 garlic clove, minced
2 tablespoons vegetable oil
1 pound lean ground beef
8 ounces bulk pork sausage
1 can (28 ounces) tomatoes
1 can (16 ounces) whole kernel corn,
     drained
1 tablespoon chili powder
½ teaspoon cumin
½ teaspoon oregano
1 cup pitted ripe olives, drained (these
     may be whole or sliced)
1 small can (7¾ ounces) tomato sauce
2 cans (15 ounces each) Nalley tamales,
     corn husks removed, cut into
     1- or 2-inch chunks
4 ounces Cheddar cheese, grated (1 cup)

Sauté onion and garlic in vegetable oil in Dutch oven or skillet until golden but not brown. Add ground beef and bulk sausage and continue sautéing until meat is brown. Drain off excess fat.

Stir in tomatoes, corn, chili powder, cumin, and oregano. Cover and simmer 10 minutes. If cooking conventionally, move mixture to 2-quart casserole dish.

Add olives, tomato sauce, and tamales. Sprinkle the top with grated Cheddar cheese.

Bake in Dutch oven for about 45 minutes, or bake uncovered in 350°F conventional oven for 45 minutes, until cheese is melted and meat mixture is bubbly.

Yield: 6 servings

RICE WITH SAUSAGE, APPLES, AND PRUNES

1½ cups uncooked wild rice
1¼ cups uncooked white rice
3 tablespoons unsalted butter
1½ cups chopped onion
6 ounces smoked sausage, cut into
    ½-inch cubes
5 cups plus 1 cup canned chicken broth
9 ounces pitted prunes, chopped
¼ teaspoon dried thyme, crumbled
¾ teaspoon salt
2 medium-sized green apples, peeled,
    cored, and cut into ½-inch pieces
salt to taste
pepper to taste

Cook wild rice in boiling water for 10 minutes. Drain and set aside. Repeat for white rice: Cook in boiling water for 10 minutes, drain, and set aside.

Melt butter in Dutch oven or large skillet, add onions, and sauté until soft. Add sausage, wild rice, and white rice, and stir. Mix in 5 cups of the chicken broth, prunes, thyme, and salt. Bring mixture to boil, stirring occasionally. Reduce heat, cover, and cook 30 minutes.

Add apples. Cover and cook until all broth is absorbed and rice is tender, adding remaining 1 cup broth if needed. Season with salt and pepper.

Yield: 6 to 8 servings

SENSATIONAL STEAK FAJITAS

¾ pound lean flank steak
2 teaspoons cumin
2 teaspoons chili powder
¼ teaspoon salt
⅛ teaspoon garlic powder
⅛ teaspoon black pepper
⅛ teaspoon ground red pepper
4 flour tortillas, 8-inch diameter
1 teaspoon canola oil
2 cups diced onion
⅓ cup green bell pepper strips
⅓ cup red bell pepper strips
⅓ cup yellow bell pepper strips
1 tablespoon lime juice
¼ cup sour cream
salsa and cilantro sprigs for garnish

Trim fat from steak. Slice diagonally across grain into thin strips. Combine steak, cumin, chili powder, salt, garlic powder, black pepper, and red pepper in a zip-top bag. Seal bag and shake well to coat.

Wrap tortillas in foil and heat in Dutch oven or warm conventional oven, or wrap in paper towels and heat in microwave.

Heat oil in skillet. Add steak, onion, and bell peppers and stir-fry for 6 minutes or until steak is medium rare. Remove from heat and add lime juice. Divide mixture among tortillas and roll up. Serve with sour cream, salsa, and cilantro.

Yield: 4 servings

SAVORY RICE AND RED BEANS

Serve this dish on its own or stuff the mixture into warm tortillas with salsa.

1 slice uncooked bacon, chopped
1 cup chopped onion
1 can (14½ ounces) chicken broth
¾ cup brown rice, unclooked
¾ cup celery, sliced
¼ teaspoon salt
¼ teaspoon hot pepper sauce
⅛ teaspoon ground black pepper
1 can (15½ ounces) dark red kidney
    beans, with liquid
1 small green bell pepper, seeded and cut
    into bite-size strips

Cook bacon until crisp. Drain bacon, reserving 1 teaspoon of the drippings. Cook onion in reserved bacon drippings until tender. Add bacon, broth, rice, celery, salt, hot pepper sauce, and pepper. Bring to boil, then reduce heat. Cover and simmer for 40 minutes.

Add kidney beans with their liquid, and pepper strips. Simmer, covered, for 5 minutes.

Yield: 6 servings

SPICY PESTO LASAGNA

2½ pounds bulk sausage
1 pound fresh pasta spfoglia sheets,
    uncooked (or 8 cooked and drained
    lasagna noodles)
2 jars (10 ounces each) pesto sauce
12 tomatoes, sliced
4 cups plain yogurt
2 pounds Monterey Jack cheese, grated
    (8 cups)
6 ounces Parmesan cheese, grated
    (2½ cups)

> *Variation: This recipe is just as delicious when made without the sausage.*

Brown sausage in Dutch oven or skillet. Drain off fat.

Arrange one layer of pasta in each of two Dutch ovens or in a 9" x 12" baking dish. Spread each layer with ¼ of the pesto (use ½ the pesto in 9" x 12" pan). Break up ¼ of the sausage (½ the sausage for 9" x 12" pan) thinly and evenly over pesto. Layer tomato slices over sausage. Spread with ½ of the yogurt and sprinkle with Monterey Jack and Parmesan. Add another layer of pasta and repeat layers of pesto, sausage, tomato slices, yogurt, and cheese. Cover top layer with sliced tomatoes and sprinkle with Parmesan.

Bake in Dutch oven 35 to 40 minutes, or bake uncovered in 350°F conventional oven for 45 to 50 minutes, until golden and bubbly. Spoon off excess olive oil. Let stand 10 minutes before serving. Cut into squares.

Yield: 10 to 15 servings

MEATLESS DISHES

REMEMBER

When a recipe calls for baking, braising, stewing, or roasting, the
Dutch oven must be covered with charcoal briquettes on top of
the lid. For boiling, frying, sautéing, and quick-heating, leave the
Dutch oven cover off. For more on cooking techniques for the
Dutch oven, see "Dutch Oven Care and Use," pages 2–3.

CRANBERRY STUFFING

My sister-in-law, Betty Mills, uses this recipe as a stuffing or side dish for fowl.

4 cups cooked wild rice
2 cups raw cranberries, coarsely chopped
½ cup butter or margarine, melted
I tablespoon grated yellow onion
3½ tablespoons sugar (optional)
½ teaspoon pepper
I teaspoon salt (optional)
½ teaspoon mace
½ teaspoon dill weed
½ teaspoon dried thyme
½ teaspoon dried marjoram
I garlic clove, minced

Combine all ingredients and pour in Dutch oven or 1½-quart casserole dish.

Cook in Dutch oven over low heat for about 10 to 15 minutes, or in 350°F conventional oven for 15 minutes, until heated through. Allow to cool if using as a stuffing.

Yield: 6 to 8 servings

TOMATO AND GARLIC PIZZA

oil for greasing pans
one recipe focaccia dough
    (recipe on page 46)
½ cup chopped fresh basil
8 garlic cloves, thinly sliced
1½ cups sliced fresh mushrooms
4 thinly sliced fresh tomatoes
freshly ground black pepper to taste
6 ounces Parmesan cheese, grated
    (1½ cups)

Grease two Dutch ovens or two pizza pans or baking sheets.

Divide the dough in half and press into two Dutch ovens or two pizza pans or baking sheets, turning the edge of the dough over on itself to form a lip. Layer basil, garlic, mushrooms, and tomatoes on top of dough. Sprinkle with pepper and Parmesan.

For Dutch oven cooking, bake for 25 minutes with about fifteen coals underneath the oven and coals covering the lid. For conventional cooking, bake in 375°F conventional oven for 20 to 25 minutes.

Yield: 2 pizzas

SWEET AND SOUR CABBAGE

Werner Rosenbaum donated this recipe, which was given to him by his mother. Most people do not care for cooked cabbage; however, Werner claims that he has never served this to anyone who has not enjoyed it and asked for seconds! This dish really complements Boomer's Salmon River Meat Rolls (recipe on page 107).

2 heads red cabbage
2 apples
1 onion, chopped
1 tablespoon caraway seeds
1 tablespoon salt
½ tablespoon pepper
2 cups water
1 cup sugar
½ cup white vinegar
8 tablespoons (1 stick) unsalted butter

Chop cabbage and apples into coarse pieces. Add onion, caraway seeds, salt, and pepper. Cook in water until cabbage is tender. Do not overcook. Drain off any remaining water. Add sugar and vinegar. Add butter and stir until melted. Serve hot.

This dish can be prepared ahead of time, frozen and reheated. If you choose this option, add the butter when reheating.

Yield: 10 servings

SWEDISH BAKED BEANS

This is a delicious recipe from my Aunt Mac in Billings, Montana.

1 apple
¼ cup raisins
¼ cup molasses
½ cup chopped onion
¾ cup catsup
1 tablespoon prepared mustard
¼ cup sweet pickle relish
¾ cup sugar
16 ounces canned baked beans (brick oven variety preferred)

Grind apple, raisins, molasses, and onion together; if you don't have access to a food processor, finely chop these ingredients. Mix well with catsup, mustard, relish, and sugar. Blend into baked beans.

Bake 1 hour in Dutch oven at medium heat, or 1½ hours in 225°F conventional oven.

Meat variation: Grind an eight-ounce piece of cooked ham in with the other ingredients.

Yield: 6 to 8 servings

TOFU CACCIATORE

This is Bill Caccia's delicious vegetarian adaptation of his brother John's Chicken Cacciatore (page 75).

several garlic cloves, sliced
1 large onion, sliced
1½ teaspoons oregano leaves
1½ teaspoons sweet basil, chopped
1 teaspoon parsley
1 teaspoon anise seeds
1 cup mushrooms, cut in half
3 tablespoons plus 1 tablespoon olive oil
1 package (14 ounces) firm tofu
3 cans (6 ounces each) tomato paste
5 cans (8 ounces each) tomato sauce
1 cup water
1 can (6 ounces) pitted black olives, drained
2 tablespoons sugar
½ teaspoon salt
½ teaspoon pepper
2 tablespoons grated Parmesan cheese
5 whole bay leaves

In a large Dutch oven, sauté garlic, onion, oregano, basil, parsley, anise seeds, and mushrooms in 3 tablespoons olive oil. Set aside.

Cut tofu into ½-inch to 1-inch cubes. In a skillet, sauté tofu in remaining 1 tablespoon oil until golden brown.

In a separate bowl, mix tomato paste, tomato sauce, water, olives, sugar, salt, pepper, Parmesan, and bay leaves. Add the tofu and the tomato sauce mixture to the Dutch oven. Simmer for 3 hours.

If you prepare the sauce ahead of time and freeze, do not prepare the tofu until the last minute.

Yield: 6 servings

PASTA FRITTATA

If you want to serve an appetizer or light entree that will delight your guests, this is the one! You may even come up with your own variation.

8 ounces uncooked spaghetti

2 tablespoons plus 1 tablespoon unsalted butter, at room temperature

8 teaspoons olive oil

½ cup finely chopped onion

1 can (32 ounces) peeled Italian plum tomatoes, chopped and drained

6 ounces mozzarella cheese, grated (1½ cups)

2 ounces Parmesan cheese, grated (½ cup)

salt and freshly ground pepper to taste

½ cup pine nuts, toasted

½ cups chopped fresh basil

5 eggs

2 teaspoons plus 2 tablespoons minced fresh Italian parsley

Cook spaghetti. Drain and mix with 2 tablespoons of the butter in a large bowl. Cool.

Heat olive oil in skillet and add onion. Cook until tender and golden brown. Add tomatoes and cook until mixture is thick. Cool to room temperature.

Stir mozzarella cheese and ½ of the Parmesan into the tomato mixture. Season with salt and pepper. Stir pine nuts and basil into tomato-cheese mixture. Set aside.

Beat five eggs in a large bowl. Stir in the spaghetti, remaining Parmesan, and 2 teaspoons of the parsley.

Heat 1 tablespoon of the butter in a 12" Dutch oven or skillet over high heat. Spread half of the pasta-egg mixture evenly in Dutch oven or pan and cook 1 minute, shaking pan to prevent sticking. Reduce heat.

Spread ⅓ of the tomato-cheese mixture over the pasta-egg mixture, leaving a ½-inch outside border. Top with remaining pasta-egg mixture, spreading to edges of pan. Cook until mixture is almost set and bottom is golden brown, about 3 to 5 minutes.

Place under broiler about 2 inches from heat, or, in Dutch oven, heat from the top only, covering the lid with briquettes as if to broil. Cook until frittata is set and golden brown. If you are making this in a skillet, invert the frittata after broiling, put it back into the skillet, and brown the other side.

Sprinkle 2 tablespoons parsley over frittata. Cut into wedges to serve. You can make this dish two hours ahead and serve it at room temperature.

Yield: 8 to 10 servings

BLACK BEAN BURRITOS

12 flour tortillas, 10-inch diameter
3 cups drained canned black beans
1½ cups finely chopped red onion
3 cups grated Monterey Jack cheese
3 avocados, peeled, pitted, and cut into
    chunks
6 tablespoons chopped cilantro
1 cup salsa

Working with one tortilla at a time, spread ¼ cup of black beans in the center. Top beans with 1 tablespoon of the onion and ¼ cup Monterey Jack. Roll tortilla gently to enclose filling. Repeat for all tortillas. Transfer the burritos, seam sides down, to a Dutch oven or 9"x 12" baking pan, forming one layer.

Bake in Dutch oven for 15 to 20 minutes, or in 350°F conventional oven for 15 to 20 minutes. Top each burrito with avocado, cilantro, and salsa.

Yield: 12 servings

HERB-BROILED TOMATOES

¾ cup shredded whole wheat cereal,
    crushed fine
1½ tablespoons minced fresh parsley
½ teaspoon dried whole basil
⅛ teaspoon garlic powder
1 tablespoon unsalted butter, melted
3 medium tomatoes
fresh parsley sprigs for garnish

Combine cereal, parsley, basil, and garlic powder in a small bowl. Add butter and stir well. Set aside.

Cut tomatoes in half crosswise. Place halves, cut side up, in a Dutch oven or baking pan. Place under broiler, or, in Dutch oven, heat from the top only, covering the lid with briquettes as if to broil, for 10 minutes. Sprinkle with cereal mixture. Broil tomatoes again until lightly browned. Garnish with parsley sprigs.

Yield: 6 servings

OLYMPIC SPUDS

I created this potato dish during the Summer Olympics and received a gold medal from my guests!

4 large Idaho baking potatoes
2 cups sour cream
4 to 6 large garlic cloves, minced
1 teaspoon freshly ground black pepper
1/4 teaspoon ground red pepper
1 teaspoon Parsley Patch seasoning,
    All-Purpose Blend (or use any salt-
    free blend of herbs)
1 bunch broccoli, chopped
1 red onion, chopped
1 pound mushrooms, chopped
ground red pepper and Parsley Patch
    seasoning to taste
4 tablespoons butter

Bake the potatoes for 45 to 60 minutes in Dutch oven, or for 1 hour in 350°F conventional oven. Cool potatoes until they can be handled.

Cut each potato in half lengthwise and scoop the insides into a bowl. Beat with sour cream, garlic, black pepper, red pepper, and 1 teaspoon Parsley Patch seasoning until fluffy and smooth. Spoon into potato shells and place in Dutch oven or 9" x 12" baking pan.

Bake in Dutch oven for 15 to 20 minutes, or in 350°F conventional oven for 15 to 20 minutes, until heated through.

Sauté broccoli, onion, mushrooms, red pepper, and Parsley Patch in butter until tender. Spoon on top of the potatoes and serve.

Yield: 8 servings

ITALIAN ZUCCHINI BAKE

1 tablespoon olive oil
1/2 cup chopped onion
3 cups shredded zucchini (squeeze out all
    excess moisture)
1 1/4 cups rolled oats
1 ounce mozzarella cheese, grated (1/4 cup)
1 egg
1/2 teaspoon dried basil, crushed
1/2 teaspoon salt (optional)
1/4 teaspoon freshly ground pepper
1/3 cup tomato sauce

Heat olive oil in 10" Dutch oven or skillet, add onion, and sauté until tender. Transfer onion to large bowl and add zucchini, oats, mozzarella cheese, egg, basil, salt, and pepper. Mix well. Pour mixture into Dutch oven or 1 1/2-quart casserole dish. Spread tomato sauce evenly over the top.

Bake in Dutch oven for 30 minutes, or in 350°F conventional oven for 30 minutes.

Yield: 6 to 8 servings

FOCACCIA AND CHÊVRE PIZZA

4 ounces mild chêvre, such as
    Montrachet, coarsely crumbled
2 tablespoons chopped fresh basil
1 baked plain focaccia, 10-inch diameter
    (recipe on page 46)
12 Kalamata olives, pitted and sliced
12 large radicchio leaves
4 teaspoons olive oil

Prepare focaccia as instructed on page 46.

Sprinkle chêvre and basil over focaccia. Top with olives and half of the radicchio leaves. Drizzle with olive oil. Place in Dutch oven or on pizza pan or baking sheet.

Heat in Dutch oven or in 350°F conventional oven for 5 to 10 minutes, until cheese melts and bread is warmed through. Top with remaining radicchio.

Yield: 6 small servings

GOOD OLD-FASHIONED DUTCH OVEN POTATOES

Neil and Carrie Dabb of Logan, Utah, shared this award-winning recipe with me. The Dabbs won first place at the World Championship Dutch Oven Cookoff in Logan in 1989.

4 slices uncooked bacon (optional), cut
    into bite-sized pieces
1 tablespoon vegetable oil (optional)
1 medium onion, sliced
5 pounds medium potatoes, sliced
½ cup chopped mushrooms
1 can (10½ ounces) cream of mushroom
    soup
½ cup sour cream
8 ounces Cheddar cheese, cubed or
    grated (2 cups)

Cook bacon in Dutch oven until nearly done (if not using bacon, preheat a small amount of oil before proceeding). Add onion and cook until light brown in color, stirring occasionally. Add potatoes and stir. Cover and let cook until potatoes are tender, about 30 minutes.

Add mushrooms, cover, and cook 3 to 5 minutes.

Add mushroom soup and sour cream. Cook 2 to 3 minutes longer.

Spread cheese on top, cover, and remove from heat. Let stand 5 to 10 minutes or until cheese melts.

Yield: 8 to 10 servings

PEPPERS STUFFED WITH GOAT CHEESE

1 red pepper
1 yellow pepper
1 green pepper
6 tablespoons butter
1 cup finely chopped onions
1 garlic clove, minced
½ cup chopped chives
12 ounces goat cheese
2 teaspoons cumin seeds
¼ teaspoon red pepper
salt and pepper to taste
½ cup pine nuts

Serve this as a meal with salsa and French bread, or alone as an appetizer.

Slice tops off red, yellow, and green pepper. Remove ribs and seeds, but leave peppers whole.

Melt butter in skillet and sauté onions and garlic until translucent. Combine with chives, goat cheese, cumin seeds, red pepper, salt, pepper, and pine nuts. Mix well. (You can also prepare this in a food processor before your camping trip. If you do so, add pine nuts at the end so they are not too finely ground.)

Stuff peppers with mixture and smooth tops with spatula. Chill for 3 hours. When stuffing is firm, cut each pepper into six slices, discarding bottoms. Put slices under broiler or in Dutch oven, stuffing-side up, with maximum heat on the top. Broil or heat until moisture begins to glaze the surface of the peppers. Serve one red, one green, and one yellow pepper for each serving.

Yield: 6 servings

SWEET CHEESE PATOOTIES

The extra-sharp Cheddar blended with mozzarella gives sweet potatoes a great taste. Try these for breakfast, too!

6 medium sweet potatoes
3 ounces extra-sharp Cheddar cheese, shredded
3 ounces mozzarella cheese, shredded
6 tablespoons raisins
6 tablespoons Grape Nuts cereal

Bake the sweet potatoes for 45 to 60 minutes in the Dutch oven or 1 hour in a 350°F conventional oven. Set aside to cool.

Cut each sweet potato in half lengthwise and scoop out pulp. Mash with a fork and put in Dutch oven or 9"x 12" baking pan. Sprinkle Cheddar cheese, mozzarella cheese, and raisins over potatoes.

Bake in Dutch oven for 3 to 5 minutes, or in 350°F conventional oven for 5 to 10 minutes, just long enough to melt cheese. Top with Grape Nuts cereal. Serve hot.

Yield: 6 servings

POLENTA WITH WILD MUSHROOMS

6½ cups water
1½ tablespoons salt
2 cups coarse-grained polenta
2 tablespoons unsalted butter
2½ tablespoons olive oil
4 shallots, peeled and minced
1 pound golden chanterelles, or other
    wild mushrooms, washed and dried
salt to taste
freshly ground pepper to taste
¼ cup chopped fresh chives
⅓ cup freshly grated Parmesan cheese

Put water and salt in a Dutch oven or saucepan; bring to a simmer. Add polenta in a thin stream, stirring constantly. Cook on low heat for about 20 minutes; polenta is ready when it pulls away from the side of the pan. Pour onto waxed paper to set up.

Heat butter and olive oil in a skillet and sauté shallots. Add chanterelles and cook until they have absorbed the butter and oil. Add salt and pepper. Cook another 15 minutes. Add chives just before mushrooms are ready.

Cut polenta in squares or wedges, and top with mushrooms and Parmesan.

The polenta can be prepared ahead of time, frozen, and reheated. To do so, freeze polenta with waxed paper between each piece. To reheat, put 1 tablespoon oil in skillet and add polenta. Turn polenta after 1 or 2 minutes and remove when heated through.

Yield: 6 servings

Desserts

REMEMBER

When a recipe calls for baking, braising, stewing, or roasting, the Dutch oven must be covered with charcoal briquettes on top of the lid. For boiling, frying, sautéing, and quick-heating, leave the Dutch oven cover off. For more on cooking techniques for the Dutch oven, see "Dutch Oven Care and Use," pages 2–3.

APPLE CRISP

butter for greasing pan

Crust:

3 cups quick oats
2 cups brown sugar
1 cup unbleached all-purpose flour
1 teaspoon baking soda
2 teaspoons salt
1 cup melted butter

Filling:

6 to 8 apples, peeled, cored, and thinly
   sliced
2 teaspoons cinnamon
2 teaspoons nutmeg

Butter Dutch oven or 9"x 12" baking pan.

Mix together well the oats, brown sugar, flour, baking soda, and salt. Add melted butter and combine.

Cover bottom of Dutch oven or pan with half of crust mixture.

Mix apples with cinnamon and nutmeg. Layer in Dutch oven or pan about 2 inches thick over bottom crust. Spread remaining crust mixture on top.

Bake for 40 to 50 minutes with coals on top of and beneath Dutch oven. For conventional cooking, bake in 350°F oven for 40 to 50 minutes.

Yield: 8 to 10 servings

ALPINE APPLE CRISP

5 medium-sized apples, cored, peeled, and
   sliced
¾ cup margarine, melted
¾ cup chopped walnuts
1½ cups rolled oats
1 teaspoon cinnamon
½ cup sunflower seeds
½ cup unbleached all-purpose flour
½ teaspoon allspice
¾ cup brown sugar
¾ cup orange juice
3 cups whipped cream (optional)

Spread half of the apples in a 10" Dutch oven or 9"x 12" baking pan.

In a separate bowl, combine margarine with walnuts, oats, cinnamon, sunflower seeds, flour, allspice, and brown sugar. Crumble half of this mixture onto apples. Layer the remaining apples, and top with the rest of the topping. Pour orange juice over top.

Bake in Dutch oven for 45 minutes, or in 375°F conventional oven for 45 minutes, until the apples are soft. Top with whipped cream if desired.

Yield: 8 servings

SUE'S APPLE RAISIN CRUMBLE

This recipe was given to me by my good friend Bill Caccia, who borrowed it from an Australian friend. He makes it in a Dutch oven on a cookstove at home, as well as over a campfire on float trips.

butter for greasing pan

Filling:

6 large apples, peeled and sliced
½ cup raisins
½ cup honey
1 teaspoon ground cinnamon

Crumble Crust:

1½ cups quick oats, uncooked
1 tablespoon sesame seeds
1 tablespoon wheat germ
¼ cup coconut
¼ cup sunflower seeds
½ cup margarine
½ cup honey

Grease a Dutch oven or 9"x 12" baking pan and set aside.

Mix apples, raisins, honey, and cinnamon. Place in Dutch oven or pan and set aside.

Make the crust: Mix oats, sesame seeds, wheat germ, coconut, and sunflower seeds. Cut in margarine and add enough honey to create a crumbly texture. Cover the apples and raisins with the crumble mixture.

Bake for 30 minutes in Dutch oven, or for 30 minutes in a 350°F conventional oven, until top is golden brown.

Yield: 8 servings

SUGARLESS APPLE TARTS

1 can (12 ounces) frozen apple juice
    concentrate
2 tablespoons butter
3 tablespoons quick-cooking tapioca
⅛ teaspoon salt
1 teaspoon ground cinnamon
½ teaspoon ground nutmeg
6 to 7 cups peeled, thinly sliced Golden
    Delicious apples
butter for greasing backs of muffin tins
pastry for a 9" double-crust pie (recipe
    on page 143)
flour for rolling out dough
3 cups whipped cream (optional)
½ cup chopped walnuts (optional)

In Dutch oven or saucepan, combine apple juice concentrate, butter, tapioca, salt, cinnamon, nutmeg, and apples. Simmer, covered and occasionally stirring gently, until apples are tender, about 10 to 15 minutes. Cool. Can be covered and chilled for up to 4 days.

Grease the back sides of 12 metal muffin cups.

Prepare pastry dough according to directions. On a floured board, roll out pastry to about ⅛ inch thick. Cut into twelve 4½-inch rounds. Drape pastry rounds over the backs of 2½ inch individual aluminum muffin cups, or over the backs of alternate cups on two standard muffin tins. Shape dough around each cup. Prick bottom of each round with fork.

Bake tart shells, bottom side up, in Dutch oven for 5 to 7 minutes, or in 450°F conventional oven for 7 to 8 minutes, until golden brown. Let tart shells cool before removing from muffin cups.

Spoon about ⅓ cup of apple filling into each tart shell. Garnish each tart with sweetened whipped cream and chopped nuts, if desired.

Yield: 12 servings

GRANDMA'S APPLE CAKE

butter for greasing pan
1½ cups plus 2 tablespoons whole wheat
    flour
5 teaspoons cornstarch
2¼ teaspoons baking soda
¾ teaspoon salt
⅛ teaspoon ground cloves
½ cup unsalted butter, diced, at room
    temperature
4 medium Gala apples, peeled, cored, and
    cut into ⅓-inch slices
¾ cup, plus 1 tablespoon packed brown
    sugar
2 large eggs
2 tablespoons milk
2 teaspoons sugar
2 tablespoons confectioner's sugar

Grease a Dutch oven or 9"x 12" baking pan and set aside.

Combine flour, cornstarch, baking soda, salt, and cloves. Cut in butter with pastry blender or fingers until mixture is the consistency of coarse cornmeal. Mix in apples and brown sugar.

In a separate bowl, whisk eggs and milk together. Stir into apple mixture to make a thick batter. Put into Dutch oven or pan and sprinkle with sugar.

Bake in Dutch oven for about 35 minutes, or in 350°F conventional oven for 35 to 45 minutes, until golden and springy to the touch. Sprinkle top with confectioner's sugar.

Yield: 8 servings

APPLESAUCE CAKE

butter for greasing pan
1½ cups honey
½ cup margarine
2 eggs
2 teaspoons baking soda
2½ cups unbleached all-purpose flour
½ teaspoon allspice
1 teaspoon ground cinnamon
1½ cups applesauce
½ cup boiling water

Grease a Dutch oven or 9"x 12" baking pan and set aside.

Mix all ingredients except water in large bowl. Add water and mix well again. Pour into Dutch oven or baking pan.

Bake in Dutch oven for 45 to 50 minutes, or in 350°F conventional oven for 45 to 55 minutes.

Yield: 15 servings

APPLE-CHEDDAR DUMPLINGS

butter for greasing pan

Pastry:

3 cups unbleached all-purpose flour
¼ cup sugar
¾ teaspoon salt
4 tablespoons chilled unsalted butter, cut
    into pieces
¼ cup chilled vegetable shortening, cut
    into pieces
1¾ cups packed, finely grated, extra-sharp
    Cheddar cheese
¾ cup ice water

Filling:

4 cups peeled, cored, and thinly sliced
    Granny Smith apples
½ cup coarsely chopped walnuts
6 tablespoons brown sugar
1 teaspoon ground cinnamon
½ teaspoon nutmeg
3 tablespoons chilled unsalted butter, cut
    into pieces

Glaze:

1 egg
1 tablespoon whipping cream

Topping:

1 cup plain yogurt or sour cream
2 tablespoons maple syrup

Grease a Dutch oven or 9"x 12" baking pan and set aside.

Make the pastry: Combine flour, sugar, and salt. Cut in butter and the shortening with a pastry blender or your fingers. Add cheese and continue to blend until mixture resembles coarse cornmeal. Mix in water until dough holds together. Knead dough briefly.

Make the filling: Combine apples, walnuts, brown sugar, cinnamon, and nutmeg. Set aside.

Make the glaze: Whip together the egg and cream. The glaze should be thick and creamy. Set aside.

Roll out dough to ¼-inch thickness. Cut into eight 3-inch squares. Place a scoop of apple filling in center of each square. Dot apple filling with remaining butter. Fold up the corners of each filled square, creating a package. Pinch edges to seal dough and brush top with glaze. Place in the bottom of Dutch oven or baking pan.

Bake in Dutch oven for about 40 minutes, or in 350°F conventional oven for 40 minutes, until crusts are golden brown.

Whisk yogurt or sour cream and syrup together and spoon over each serving.

Yield: 8 servings

STREUSELY BAKED APPLES

12 pitted dates
3 large apples, cored and cut in half
½ cup sugar
½ cup unbleached all-purpose flour
¼ teaspoon ground cinnamon
¼ teaspoon ground cardamom
3 tablespoons butter
1 cup light cream

Line a Dutch oven or 9"x 12" baking pan with parchment paper, extending paper 2 inches up sides.

Place 2 dates in the hollow of each apple half.

Stir together the sugar, flour, cinnamon, and cardamom. Add butter and blend mixture with your fingers or a pastry blender. Using your fingers, pack mixture tightly in a mound over date-filled side of each apple half. Place apples, filling side up, in Dutch oven or pan.

Bake in Dutch oven for 15 to 20 minutes, or in a 350°F oven for 30 minutes, until apples are tender. Pass light cream to serve with fruit.

Yield: 3 to 6 servings

APRICOT-RAISIN BARS

butter for greasing pan

Filling:

½ cup dried apricots, diced
¼ cup raisins
½ cup apples, peeled and grated
½ cup apricot preserves

Crust:

1½ teaspoons baking soda
1 cup unbleached all-purpose flour
½ cup oat bran
2 cups rolled oats
1 teaspoon ground cinnamon
1 cup brown sugar
¾ cup margarine, melted

Grease a 12" Dutch oven or 9"x 12" baking pan and set aside.

Make the filling: In a medium-sized bowl, combine apricots, raisins, apples, and apricot preserves. Stir well and set aside.

Make the crust: In a large bowl, combine baking soda, flour, oat bran, oats, cinnamon, and brown sugar. Stir in melted margarine.

Press slightly more than half of crust mixture in bottom of Dutch oven or pan. Spread filling mixture over crust. Sprinkle remaining crust on top.

Bake in Dutch oven for 20 minutes, or in 350°F conventional oven for 20 to 25 minutes.

Yield: 24 bars

APRICOT UPSIDE-DOWN SKILLET CAKE

Tawna Skinner, a Salmon River entrepreneur and organic gardener extraordinaire, shared this mouth-watering recipe with me.

3 tablespoons butter
⅓ cup plus ⅔ cup honey
2 cups halved fresh apricots
¼ cup chopped almonds
½ cup margarine or oil
2 eggs
I teaspoon vanilla extract
½ teaspoon baking soda
¼ cup yogurt or buttermilk
1¾ cups whole wheat pastry flour
3 cups whipped cream or sour cream

Melt butter over low heat in bottom of heavy skillet or Dutch oven. Stir in ⅓ cup honey. Simmer until well mixed and slightly thickened. If cooking conventionally, pour mixture into 9"x 9" baking pan.

Arrange apricots, cut-side down, over mixture. Cover with almonds.

In large bowl, blend margarine or oil and remaining ⅔ cup honey. Beat in eggs one at a time until blended. Add vanilla.

In a small bowl, combine baking soda and yogurt or buttermilk. Add to egg mixture. Add flour and mix well. The batter should be rather thin. Pour batter over apricots.

Bake in Dutch oven over medium heat for 30 to 40 minutes, or in 250°F conventional oven for 40 to 50 minutes. Remove from pan immediately by inverting a large plate over skillet or Dutch oven and turning whole assembly upside down. Serve warm or cold topped with whipped cream or sour cream.

Yield: 8 to 10 servings

CAMEL GULCH CARROT CAKE

Camel Gulch is a drainage gulch on the Salmon River in Idaho. It is named for the Camel family, who lived at the mouth of the river in the days of Idaho's earliest settlers.

butter for greasing pan
2 cups unbleached all-purpose flour
1½ teaspoons baking soda
2 teaspoons baking powder
1 teaspoon salt
2 teaspoons ground cinnamon
2 cups sugar
1½ cups vegetable oil
4 eggs
2 cups grated carrots
1 can (8 ounces) crushed pineapple, drained
1 cup flaked coconut
½ cup chopped walnuts

Lightly butter a 12" Dutch oven or 9"x 12" baking pan.

In a large bowl combine flour, baking soda, baking powder, salt, and cinnamon. Stir in sugar, vegetable oil, eggs, carrots, pineapple, coconut, and walnuts. Pour batter into Dutch oven or pan.

Bake in Dutch oven for 30 to 40 minutes, or in 350°F conventional oven for 45 to 55 minutes. Let cool and frost with Cream Cheese Frosting (recipe follows).

Yield: 12 to 15 servings

CREAM CHEESE FROSTING

8 ounces cream cheese, softened
½ cup unsalted butter
1 teaspoon vanilla extract
⅓ cup confectioner's sugar

Combine cream cheese, butter, and vanilla; beat until fluffy. Gradually add the confectioner's sugar. Beat again until smooth.

PASTRY CRUST FOR DOUBLE-CRUST PIE

This recipe makes enough dough for an 8", 9", or 10" double-crust pie. For recipes requiring a single-crust pastry shell, simply cut these ingredients in half.

2 cups unbleached all-purpose flour
1 teaspoon salt
⅔ cup shortening
5 to 7 tablespoons cold water

Mix flour and salt. Cut in shortening with pastry blender or fork until pieces are the size of small peas. Sprinkle water over mixture. Gently toss with a fork until moist.

Divide dough for top and bottom crusts and form into two balls. Flatten on lightly floured surface. Roll from center out to ⅛-inch thickness.

Fold dough into quarters and lift into Dutch oven or pie plate. Shape edges as desired. Proceed with pie recipe instructions.

(For single-crust pies requiring a pre-baked crust, bake in Dutch oven for 10 to 12 minutes, or in 450°F conventional oven for 10 to 12 minutes.)

CHERRY PIE

pastry for a 10" double-crust pie (recipe on page 143)
3 cups tart, fresh red cherries, pitted
1 cup sugar
¼ cup unbleached all-purpose flour
dash salt
2 tablespoons butter, chilled and cut into pieces

Line the bottom of a 10" Dutch oven with prepared pastry shell, or place pie tin with pastry shell directly in the bottom of the Dutch oven. If baking conventionally, place prepared pastry shell in 10" pie dish.

Combine cherries, sugar, flour, and salt. Pour into pastry shell and dot with butter. Cover with second pastry shell and seal, crimping edges. Bake in Dutch oven for 40 to 45 minutes, or in 350°F conventional oven for 40 to 45 minutes. Let cool before slicing.

Yield: 8 servings

BLACKBERRY COBBLER

Filling:
⅔ cup sugar
2 tablespoons unbleached all-purpose flour
4 cups fresh or thawed frozen blackberries (16 ounces)

Crust:
½ cup unbleached all-purpose flour
1 teaspoon baking powder
½ cup whole wheat flour
1½ tablespoons butter or margarine, chilled
6 tablespoons milk
flour for rolling out dough

Make the filling: Combine sugar and 2 tablespoons flour. Add blackberries. Pour into a 10" Dutch oven or 9"x 9" baking dish, and set aside.

Make the crust: Mix ½ cup flour, baking powder, and whole wheat flour. Cut in butter or margarine with pastry blender or fingers until mixture resembles coarse crumbs. Stir in milk to make a soft dough and knead lightly until smooth. Put dough on a floured board and roll out to an 11-inch circle.

Place dough over berries, trimming to fit. Cut slits in dough for steam to escape.

Bake in Dutch oven for 20 to 30 minutes, or in 350°F conventional oven for 25 to 35 minutes, or until crust is browned and filling is bubbly.

Yield: 6 servings

BAKED BLACKBERRY ROLLUPS

¼ cup butter, melted
1 cup water
1 cup plus 3 tablespoons sugar
1½ cups self-rising cake flour
¼ cup unsalted butter, chilled
⅓ cup milk
flour for rolling out dough
½ teaspoon ground cinnamon
3 cups fresh or thawed frozen
    blackberries

Line a 10" Dutch oven or 9"x 9" baking pan with parchment paper.

In a saucepan, combine melted butter, water, and 1 cup of the sugar and heat until sugar is dissolved.

Cut chilled butter into flour with pastry blender or fingers until it resembles coarse cornmeal. Add milk and stir just until dough forms. Put dough on a floured board and roll out into an 11"x 9" rectangle. Sprinkle dough with cinnamon and scatter blackberries over the top.

Beginning at the long side, roll dough up jelly-roll fashion. Cut rolled dough into 1½-inch slices. Arrange slices (they will be messy), cut-side up, in Dutch oven or pan. Pour sugar syrup over slices.

Bake for 40 minutes in Dutch oven or 350°F conventional oven. Sprinkle 3 tablespoons sugar over the top and bake 15 more minutes or until golden brown.

Yield: 6 servings

BLUEBERRY-APPLE CRUMBLE

Impress your friends with this colorful, delicious dessert.

butter for greasing pan
    (unless using parchment)

Filling:

7½ cups frozen blueberries (16 ounces)
7 cups peeled, chopped Granny Smith
    apples
2 teaspoons lemon zest
1 tablespoon fresh lemon juice
½ cup unbleached all-purpose flour
¾ cup sugar
⅓ cup packed brown sugar
1¾ teaspoons ground cinnamon

Topping:

1 cup quick-cooking oats
⅓ cup unbleached all-purpose flour
¾ cup packed brown sugar
pinch salt
2 tablespoons chilled butter, cut into pieces
2 tablespoons canola oil

Butter a Dutch oven or 9"x 12" baking pan, or line with parchment paper, extending paper two inches up sides.

Make the filling: Combine blueberries, apples, lemon zest, and lemon juice. In a separate bowl, stir together flour, sugars, and cinnamon. Stir the two mixtures together and place in Dutch oven or pan. Bake in Dutch oven or 350°F conventional oven for 20 minutes.

Make the topping: Combine oats, flour, brown sugar, and salt. Cut in butter with a pastry blender or with fingers. Stir in oil. Sprinkle topping evenly over fruit.

Bake for 30 to 40 more minutes until top is brown and fruit is bubbly.

Yield: 16 servings

STRAWBERRY YOGURT CHEESECAKE

Crust:

¼ cup honey
8 tablespoons margarine, melted
2 cups graham crackers, crushed

Filling:

8 ounces cream cheese, softened
2 teaspoons vanilla extract
2 cups plain yogurt
¼ cup honey
¼ teaspoon salt
2 eggs

1 quart fresh strawberries, sliced

Prepare the crust: Stir margarine and honey together and mix with crackers. Press crust firmly into 10" metal pie tin (or you can use a glass pan if baking this in a conventional oven). If making in Dutch oven, place pie tin inside Dutch oven.

Beat cream cheese with vanilla until creamy. Add the yogurt, honey, and salt, and mix well. Add eggs one at a time, mixing just until blended. Pour mixture into shell.

Bake in Dutch oven or in 350°F conventional oven for about 1 hour, or until firm. Let cool and top with sliced strawberries. Chill at least one hour before serving.

Yield: 8 servings

RASPBERRY BREAD PUDDING

butter for greasing pan

Pudding:

2 cups milk
½ cup sugar
¼ teaspoon nutmeg
1 teaspoon vanilla extract
3 eggs, lightly beaten
3 cups day-old Italian or French bread, cut in 1-inch cubes
4 tablespoons butter, melted
1 cup raspberries, fresh or frozen
1 tablespoon confectioner's sugar

Raspberry Sauce:

1 cup raspberries, fresh or frozen
2 tablespoons confectioner's sugar
3 cups whipped cream

Grease a Dutch oven or 9"x 12" baking pan and set aside.

Bring milk just to a boil, remove from heat, and stir in sugar. Add nutmeg and vanilla and let cool for 10 minutes. Whisk in eggs.

In a separate bowl, toss bread cubes with melted butter. Pour bread mixture into Dutch oven or pan and spoon berries over top. Pour milk and egg mixture over bread mixture.

Bake in Dutch oven or in 350°F conventional oven for 1 hour, until set and starting to brown. Let cool. Dust with 1 tablespoon confectioner's sugar.

Make raspberry sauce: Push the remaining 1 cup raspberries through a sieve. Mix resulting juice with 2 tablespoons confectioner's sugar. Cook over medium heat, stirring until sugar is completely dissolved. Pour sauce over the cake and serve cake with whipped cream.

Yield: 6 servings

GLAZED PEACH PIE

pastry for a 10" single-crust pie
    (recipe on page 143)
5 cups sliced fresh peaches
¾ cup fructose or granulated sugar
3 tablespoons unbleached all-purpose
    flour
½ teaspoon nutmeg
¼ teaspoon salt
1 teaspoon lemon juice
¼ teaspoon almond extract
¼ cup apricot preserves

Prepare pastry dough. Form it into a deep-dish crust in Dutch oven or pie tin (you may place metal pie tin inside Dutch oven). Preheat lid to Dutch oven or, if using a conventional oven, preheat to 425°F.

Toss together peaches, fructose or sugar, flour, nutmeg, salt, lemon juice, and almond extract. Arrange two circles of peach slices, all pointing to center, over the bottom of the crust. Top with two more layers of peach slices arranged in the same way.

Bake pie in Dutch oven or in 425°F conventional oven for 15 to 20 minutes, then cover with foil and bake 15 to 20 minutes longer until peaches are fork-tender.

Melt apricot preserves and brush over peaches.

Yield: 8 servings

DELIGHTFUL PEACHES

6 medium peaches, pitted and cut into
    eighths
¼ cup Grand Marnier liqueur
1½ cup crushed amaretti cookies (Italian
    macaroons), or almond macaroons
½ cup finely chopped toasted almonds
1 tablespoon unsweetened cocoa powder
¼ cup chilled unsalted butter, sliced
3 cups whipped cream or vanilla ice
    cream

Arrange peaches in a 10" Dutch oven or 9"x 9" baking dish. Pour Grand Marnier over peaches and toss gently. Let peach mixture stand for 30 minutes.

Combine cookies, almonds, and cocoa powder in small bowl. Add butter and rub mixture with fingertips until mixture resembles coarse cornmeal. Sprinkle over peaches.

Bake in Dutch oven for about 20 minutes, or in 350°F conventional oven for 20 to 25 minutes, until peaches are tender and topping is brown. Cool slightly. Serve with whipped cream or vanilla ice cream.

Yield: 6 servings

PEACH CRUMB FLAN

Crust:

6 tablespoons unsalted butter
I cup whole wheat flour
¼ cup honey

Filling:

8 ounces Neufchâtel or light cream
    cheese, softened
2 tablespoons plus 4 tablespoons honey
I egg
½ teaspoon vanilla extract
4 cups sliced, peeled fresh peaches (or
    use canned peaches, drained)
½ teaspoon cinnamon
¼ cup sliced almonds

Make the crust: Cut the butter into the flour. Add ¼ cup honey, and mix. Pat the mixture into the bottom of a Dutch oven or 9"x 12" baking pan, extending the crust 1½ inches up the sides. Bake crust in Dutch oven or in 350°F conventional oven for 8 to 10 minutes.

Make the filling: Mix the Neufchâtel or cream cheese and 2 tablespoons of the honey until smooth. Add egg and vanilla, and blend well. Pour filling into crust.

In a separate bowl, toss the peaches with the remaining 4 tablespoons honey and cinnamon until evenly coated. Spoon peaches onto cream cheese mixture. Sprinkle almonds on top.

Bake in Dutch oven for 25 to 35 minutes, or in 350°F conventional oven for 30 to 35 minutes, or until the almonds are lightly toasted.

Yield: 8 servings

PEAR-CRANBERRY COBBLER

This is a simple but absolutely delicious Dutch oven dessert.

Butter a 12" Dutch oven or 9"x 12" baking pan.

butter for greasing pan

Crust:

2½ cups unbleached all-purpose flour
1 teaspoon salt
10 tablespoons unsalted butter
⅔ cup chilled vegetable shortening
½ cup ice water
butter for greasing pan
flour for rolling out dough

Filling:

7 cups cranberries (24 ounces)
8 pears, peeled and sliced
1 cup sugar
½ cup unbleached all-purpose flour
½ teaspoon ground allspice
¼ teaspoon ground cardamom
6 cups ice cream or whipped cream
    (optional)

Make the crust: Mix 2½ cups flour and salt. Cut butter and shortening into flour with pastry blender or fingers until it forms pea-sized lumps. Add water, working mixture as little as possible until dough is formed. Wrap dough in plastic and chill for 20 minutes.

Sprinkle cranberries and pears with sugar, ½ cup flour, allspice, and cardamom. Mix well. Spread mixture in Dutch oven or pan. Put pastry on a floured board and roll out to ⅛-inch thickness, in a round 1 inch larger than pan.

Fold dough in half to place on top of fruit. Unfold carefully and crimp edges decoratively. Cut slits in top.

Bake in Dutch oven for 35 to 40 minutes, or in 350°F conventional oven for 50 to 60 minutes, until crust is golden brown and bubbly and cranberries have split. Cool 15 minutes and serve with ice cream or whipped cream.

Yield: 12 servings

RUBY RAPID RHUBARB PIE

This is a recipe that my mother, Jane McDonald, adapted to a Dutch oven and renamed on the Main Salmon River.

Crust:

1 cup unbleached all-purpose flour
⅓ cup confectioner's sugar
½ cup margarine

Filling:

2 eggs, beaten
1½ cups sugar
¼ cup unbleached all-purpose flour
¾ teaspoon salt
2 cups finely chopped rhubarb

Make the crust: Mix 1 cup flour, confectioner's sugar, and margarine. Press into the bottom of Dutch oven or 9"x 12" baking pan. Bake in Dutch oven or in 375°F conventional oven for 15 minutes, being careful not to burn the bottom.

Mix eggs, sugar, ¼ cup flour, salt, and rhubarb. Spread rhubarb mixture on top of the crust.

Bake in Dutch oven for 30 minutes, or in 350°F conventional oven for 30 minutes. Let stand 15 minutes before serving.

Yield: 8 to 10 servings

RHUBARB CAKE

butter for greasing pan
½ cup margarine
1½ cups brown sugar, or 1 cup honey
2 eggs
1 teaspoon baking soda
1 cup sour cream
2 cups sifted flour, unbleached all-purpose
    or wheat
1½ cups diced rhubarb
1 teaspoon vanilla extract
½ cup chopped nuts
½ cup sugar
1 teaspoon cinnamon
2 tablespoons butter

Grease a 9"x 13" pan or 12" Dutch oven and set aside.

Cream margarine and sugar or honey. Add eggs and blend well.

In a separate bowl, combine baking soda and sour cream. Add to creamed mixture alternately with flour and blend well. Add rhubarb, vanilla, and nuts. Pour batter into pan.

In a small bowl, blend sugar, cinnamon, and butter. Sprinkle on top of batter.

Bake in Dutch oven for 30 to 40 minutes, or in 350°F conventional oven for 30 to 40 minutes.

Yield: 10 to 12 servings

REDSIDE RHUBARB

"Redside" is both another name for cutthroat trout and the name of a rapid on the Salmon River.

3 cups diced rhubarb (preferably straw-
berry rhubarb, a sweet red variety)
2 tablespoons orange juice
⅓ cup plus ¼ cup honey
1 tablespoon butter
1 egg, beaten
1 teaspoon vanilla extract
2 tablespoons sour cream
1 cup pastry flour
¼ teaspoon salt
½ teaspoon baking soda

Line a 10" Dutch oven or 9"x 9" baking pan with parchment paper, extending paper 2 inches up sides. Arrange rhubarb on paper.

In a small bowl, mix orange juice and ⅓ cup honey. Drizzle over rhubarb. Dot with butter.

In another bowl, combine egg, ¼ cup honey, vanilla, and sour cream. In a separate bowl, mix flour, salt, and soda; add to egg mixture. Spread resulting batter over rhubarb.

Bake in Dutch oven for about 30 minutes, or in 350°F conventional oven for 30 minutes, or until browned.

Yield: 6 servings

SOUR CREAM RAISIN PIE

My sister-in-law, Angie Mills, uses her grandmother's "no-fail pie crust" for this special dessert.

Crust:

1 cup unbleached all-purpose flour, or
    ¾ cup whole wheat flour
dash of salt
½ cup shortening
¼ cup water
flour for rolling out dough

Filling:

½ cup plus ¼ cup water
1½ cups raisins
2 eggs
1 pint sour cream
1 teaspoon lemon juice or vinegar
pinch of salt
¾ cup sugar
2 tablespoons cornstarch

Make the crust: Mix flour and salt and cut in shortening with pastry blender or fingers. Add ¼ cup water and blend until a dough is formed. Roll out on floured board, put in Dutch oven or pie plate, and trim and crimp edges. Chill for 15 minutes.

Bake crust in Dutch oven or in 450°F conventional oven for 10 to 15 minutes, or until brown.

Heat ½ cup water to boiling, pour over raisins, and let stand 5 minutes until raisins are plump.

Beat eggs and add sour cream, lemon juice or vinegar, salt, and sugar. Add to raisin mixture. Mix cornstarch with ¼ cup water and add to mixture. Cook over medium heat until it boils. Pour into prebaked pie shell. Let cool.

Yield: 6 servings

CORNY LEMON CAKE

yellow cornmeal for dusting parchment
1 cup yellow cornmeal
½ cup unbleached all-purpose flour
1½ teaspoons baking powder
¼ teaspoon salt
1 cup sugar
¼ cup canola oil
2 tablespoons butter, softened
2 large eggs
2 egg whites
½ cup plain yogurt
1½ tablespoons lemon zest
1 tablespoon fresh lemon juice
½ teaspoon lemon extract
1 cup assorted fresh or frozen thawed
    berries
¼ cup creme de cassis liqueur

Line a Dutch oven or 9"x 12" baking pan with parchment paper, extending paper 2 inches up sides. Dust with cornmeal and set aside.

Mix together 1 cup cornmeal, flour, baking powder, and salt, and set aside.

In a separate bowl, whisk together sugar, oil, and butter until well combined. Add eggs and egg whites, one at a time, until blended.

In a small bowl, stir together yogurt, lemon zest, lemon juice, and lemon extract. Fold into sugar-egg mixture until just combined. Fold lemon mixture into dry ingredients until just combined. Do not overmix. Pour batter into Dutch oven or pan and smooth the top with a spatula or knife.

Bake in Dutch oven for about 40 minutes, or in 350°F conventional oven for 40 to 45 minutes, or until toothpick inserted in center comes out clean.

Toss berries with liqueur. Cut cake into wedges and serve, topped with berries.

Yield: 12 servings

LEMON BARS

My mother's good friend Martha Kraus, from Sun City, shared this delightfully rich dessert with her.

½ cup melted butter
½ cup plus 2 tablespoons unbleached all-purpose flour
1¼ cups sugar
½ teaspoon baking powder
2 beaten eggs
2 tablespoons lemon juice
2 tablespoons additional lemon juice (optional)
¼ cup confectioner's sugar (optional)

Mix butter, ½ cup flour, and sugar. Pat into a 10" Dutch oven or 8"x 8" baking pan. Bake in Dutch oven or 350°F conventional oven for 15 minutes.

Mix remaining 2 tablespoons flour, baking powder, eggs, and lemon juice and pour over the crust.

Bake in Dutch oven or 350°F conventional oven for 25 minutes. Do not brown the top.

If desired, make a glaze of 2 tablespoons lemon juice and ¼ cup confectioner's sugar, and frost bars while warm. Or, sprinkle with confectioner's sugar. Cool and cut into squares.

Yield: 12 bars

UNBEATABLE PECAN BROWNIES

butter for greasing pan
4 ounces unsweetened chocolate
¼ cup plus ¾ cup plus 2 tablespoons unsalted butter, softened
1¾ cups sugar
3 large eggs
1 cup chopped pecans, lightly toasted
2½ tablespoons sour cream
1 tablespoon dark rum
pinch ground cinnamon
1 cup unbleached all-purpose flour, sifted

Butter a 12" Dutch oven or 9"x 13" pan.

Melt chocolate and ¼ cup butter over low heat, stirring until smooth. Let cool completely.

Cream remaining butter and sugar; beat until light and fluffy. Add eggs, one at a time, beating well after each. Beat in chocolate-butter mixture. Stir in pecans, sour cream, rum, cinnamon, and flour. Pour the batter into Dutch oven or pan, smoothing the top with a spatula or knife.

Bake in Dutch oven for 30 to 40 minutes, or in 350°F conventional oven for 30 to 40 minutes, or until batter pulls away from the sides of the pan slightly and a wooden pick inserted in the center comes out with crumbs clinging to it. Let cake cool before cutting.

Yield: 24 brownies

DEVIL'S TOOTH CHEESECAKE

This dessert is served by Kurt and Gail Selisch of Middle Fork River Tours. It is named after Devil's Tooth Rapid.

Crust:

4 tablespoons butter, melted
1 package chocolate cookie wafers, crushed

Filling:

16 ounces cream cheese, softened
1 cup sugar
16 ounces ricotta cheese
6 eggs
½ cup sour cream
12 ounces semisweet chocolate chips
¼ cup butter
½ cup whipping cream
1½ teaspoons almond flavoring
1½ teaspoons vanilla extract

Make the crust: Blend the butter with the cookie crumbs and press mixture into a 10" Dutch oven or springform pan. Press the dough up the sides of pan at least 1 inch. Set aside.

Mix cream cheese, sugar, ricotta, eggs, and sour cream until smooth. Set aside.

Melt chocolate chips, butter, and whipping cream over low heat until smooth. Add almond flavoring. Pour one third of the cheese mixture into chocolate mixture, and mix well. Pour this into crust. Add vanilla to remaining cheese mixture and carefully pour this over the chocolate layer.

Bake in Dutch oven or 350°F conventional oven for about 1¼ hours, or until the top cracks and the cake is firm. Serve warm or chilled.

Yield: 10 to 12 servings

ELVERA'S SOURDOUGH CHOCOLATE CAKE

½ cup Sourdough Starter
    (recipe on page 48)
1 cup warm water
1½ cups unbleached all-purpose flour
¼ cup powdered milk
butter for greasing pans
1 cup sugar
½ cup vegetable shortening
½ teaspoon salt
1½ teaspoons baking soda
1 teaspoon ground cinnamon
1 teaspoon vanilla extract
2 eggs
3 squares (1 ounce each) unsweetened
    chocolate, melted

Mix starter, warm water, flour, and milk and let ferment 2 to 3 hours in a warm place until mixture is bubbly and smells sour.

Grease a 10" Dutch oven or two round layer pans.

Cream sugar, shortening, salt, soda, cinnamon, and vanilla thoroughly. Add eggs one at a time, beating well after each addition.

Melt chocolate over low heat. Combine creamed mixture and melted chocolate with sourdough mixture. Stir 300 strokes by hand or in mixer on low speed until blended. Pour into Dutch oven or two layer pans.

Bake in Dutch oven for 25 to 30 minutes, or in 350°F conventional oven for 25 to 30 minutes. Cool before frosting with your favorite icing.

Yield: 12 servings

YOGURT CHOCOLATE CAKE

butter for greasing pan
flour for dusting pan
1 egg, lightly beaten
⅔ cup plus 1 cup sugar
½ cup milk
3 squares (1 ounce each) unsweetened
    chocolate
½ cup shortening
1 teaspoon vanilla extract
2 eggs
2 cups cake flour
1 teaspoon baking soda
½ teaspoon salt
1 cup plain or fruit yogurt
confectioner's sugar (optional)

Grease and flour a Dutch oven or 9" x 12" cake pan and
set aside.

In a saucepan, combine egg, ⅔ cup sugar, milk, and
unsweetened chocolate. Cook, stirring, over medium heat until
chocolate melts and mixture just begins to boil. Set aside to cool.

In a separate bowl, cream 1 cup sugar and shortening
until light and fluffy. Add vanilla. Add eggs, one at a time,
beating well after each.

In a separate bowl, sift together cake flour, baking soda,
and salt. Add flour mixture to creamed mixture alternately
with yogurt, beating after each addition. Blend in chocolate
mixture. Pour in Dutch oven or cake pan.

Bake in Dutch oven for 20 to 25 minutes, or in 350°F conventional oven for 25 to 30 minutes. Let cool, and frost with
your favorite frosting or sprinkle with confectioner's sugar.

Yield: 12 servings

GINGERBREAD CAKE

¼ cup sugar
½ cup milk
¼ cup molasses
¼ cup melted margarine
2 tablespoons honey
I egg white
I cup unbleached all-purpose flour
I teaspoon ground ginger
I teaspoon ground cinnamon
¾ teaspoon baking soda
¼ teaspoon salt
¼ teaspoon ground cloves
I tablespoon confectioner's sugar
3 cups whipped cream or ice cream
    (optional)

Line a 10" Dutch oven or 9"x 9" baking pan with parchment paper, extending paper 2 inches up sides.

Combine sugar, milk, molasses, margarine, honey, and egg white, and beat until smooth. Set aside.

In a separate bowl, combine flour, ginger, cinnamon, baking soda, salt, and cloves. Stir well. Mix wet and dry mixtures together, beating well. Pour batter into Dutch oven or pan.

Bake in Dutch oven for 25 minutes, or in 350°F conventional oven for 25 to 35 minutes, or until toothpick inserted in center comes out clean. Sprinkle with confectioner's sugar. Can be served with whipped cream or ice cream.

Yield: 6 servings

WAR CAKE

My sister-in-law Angie Mills's mother made this cake during World War II when groceries were in short supply. She called it "eggless, butterless, milkless cake."

butter for greasing pan
flour for dusting pan
2 cups water
2 cups sugar
I cup shortening
2 cups raisins
I cup walnuts, optional
½ teaspoon ground cloves
I teaspoon ground cinnamon
2 cups unbleached all-purpose flour
¼ teaspoon allspice
2 teaspoons baking soda

Grease and flour a Dutch oven or 9"x 12" cake pan and set aside.

Combine water, sugar, shortening, raisins, walnuts, cloves, and cinnamon in a saucepan. Bring to a boil and cool. Add enough flour to stiffen mixture. Add allspice and baking soda.

Bake in Dutch oven for 30 minutes, or in 325°F conventional oven for 30 minutes, or until center springs back when touched.

Yield: 12 servings

OATMEAL CAKE

My mother often baked this moist and yummy cake when I was growing up.

Cake:

butter for greasing pan
flour for dusting pan
1¼ cups boiling water
1 cup rolled oats
1 cup white sugar
1 cup brown sugar
½ cup butter or margarine
2 eggs
1⅓ cups unbleached all-purpose flour
1 teaspoon baking soda
½ teaspoon ground cinnamon
½ teaspoon salt
1 teaspoon vanilla extract

Topping:

1 cup brown sugar
3 tablespoons melted butter
6 tablespoons cream
1 cup shredded coconut
1 cup chopped nuts

Grease and flour a 12" Dutch oven or 9"x 13" pan and set aside.

Pour boiling water over oats and let stand while mixing the rest of the cake.

Cream together sugars and butter or margarine. Add eggs and mix well.

In a separate bowl, sift together flour, soda, cinnamon, and salt. Add to sugar mixture. Stir in oatmeal mixture and vanilla. Pour batter into Dutch oven or pan.

Bake in Dutch oven for 30 minutes, or in 350°F conventional oven for 30 to 40 minutes.

Make the topping: Mix brown sugar, melted butter, cream, coconut, and nuts. Pour topping over partly cooled cake and place under broiler for a few minutes until brown and bubbly.

Yield: 12 servings

IMPOSSIBLY POSSIBLE DUTCH OVEN ICE CREAM

1 small package (3.4 ounces) instant pudding (any flavor)
2 cups milk
½ cup sugar
1 egg
½ tablespoon vanilla extract
¼ teaspoon lemon juice
1 cup whipping cream
1 can (12 ounces) evaporated milk

Neil and Carrie Dabb submitted this winner at the World Championship Dutch Oven Cookoff in Logan, Utah.

Chill a 12" Dutch oven in a cooler or refrigerator.

Mix pudding and milk. In a separate bowl, mix sugar, egg, vanilla, and lemon juice. Add to pudding mixture.

Pour mixture into a dry and very cool Dutch oven. Add whipping cream and evaporated milk; stir. Put lid on Dutch oven. Place oven in a 16" bowl. Arrange crushed ice and rock salt around oven as you would in an ice cream freezer (alternating 1-inch layers of ice and ¼-inch to ½-inch layers of salt). Placing ice on the lid (no deeper than the lip) will cool the oven down faster.

Lift the lid and stir every 2 to 5 minutes. It will go slowly at first until the oven cools off. Add ice and salt to bowl as needed. Total freezing time is 30 to 45 minutes. The ice cream may be eaten soft, or if you prefer harder ice cream, you may replace the lid and cover it with ice and salt.

Note: Any ice cream recipe may be frozen with this method; however, a cooked ice cream may pick up a unique flavor from the cast iron of the oven. If a cooked recipe is used, make sure the oven is well cooled before placing it in the ice (a hot oven could crack or shatter if placed directly in the ice).

Yield: 8 to 10 servings

WHERE TO BUY

Aluminum Dutch ovens in 10" and 12" sizes can be purchased from the following sources:

Andy & Bax
   324 SE Grand Avenue
   Portland, OR 97214
   (503) 234-7538

Blackadar Boating
   P.O. Box 1170
   Salmon, ID 83467
   (208) 756-3958

Cascade Outfitters
   145 Pioneer Parkway East
   Springfield, OR 97477
   (800) 223-7238

Expedition, Inc.
   625 North Beaver Street
   Flagstaff, AZ 86001
   (520) 779-3769

Midwest Mountaineering
   309 Cedar Avenue South
   Minneapolis, MN 55464
   (612) 339-3433

Pacific River Supplies
   3675 San Pablo Dam Road
   El Sobrante, CA 94803
   (510) 223-3675

Scott Manufacturing Company
   2525 Monroe Avenue
   Cleveland, OH 44113
   (216) 579-1266

The cast-iron models often are available at hardware stores and outdoor retailers. The largest manufacturer is:

Lodge Manufacturing Company
   P.O. Box 380
   South Pittsburgh, TN 46342
   (423) 837-7181

Become a member of the International Dutch Oven Society by writing:

International Dutch Oven Society
   % Dick Machaud
   1104 Thrushwood
   Logan, UT 84321
   (801) 752-2631

Katadyn water purifiers can be purchased through most whitewater equipment stores and catalogs. Some good sources are:

Eastern Mountain Sports
  all locations
  (603) 356-9571

L.L. Bean
  Freeport, ME 04033
  (800) 221-4221

Northwest River Supplies
  P.O. Box 9186
  Moscow, ID 83843
  (800) 635-5205

REI
  all locations
  (800) 426-4840

Firepans can be purchased through Northwest River Supplies and from:

Cambridge Welding & Bending
  P.O. Box 272
  Cambridge, ID 83610
  (208) 257-3589

INDEX